I0627006

Roy Dean

Becoming the Black Belt

Becoming the Black Belt

©2016, 2025 Roy Dean

ISBN: eBook 979-8-9901327-0-2

ISBN: paperback 979-8-9901327-1-9

First edition: February 2016

Second edition: May 2025

Printed in the USA

DEDICATION

For everyone who believed in me.

Thank you.

Table of Contents

FOREWORD

I am honored to write this forward for Mr. Roy Dean. He is a good friend of mine and a very talented individual!

Our friendship and Jiu Jitsu journey began in the early 2000's. Mr. Dean, in his long and lanky frame, came strutting into the Jiu Jitsu class I was teaching at the Main Gym on the UCSD campus. During class, he presented his smooth and flowing style of Jiu Jitsu mixed with his wild, wavy, bushy hair and his cool, calm and relaxed demeanor. I distinctly remember those beginning days.

After spending a couple of semesters in my Jiu Jitsu classes at the University, he wanted more. So, he began training with my students and I at the Harris Academy in Miramar, California.

Mr. Dean came to me ranked as a blue belt belt in Brazilian Jiu Jitsu. With two years of group and private training under his belt, he took my purple belt examination and passed with flying colors. His smooth and fluid style was progressing and growing stronger with each passing year.

After having taken a couple of my week-long instructor courses, Roy began teaching group classes at my academy. He excelled at teaching right from the start.

In 2004, Roy came to me and requested to test for the rank of brown belt in Brazilian Jiu Jitsu. Anyone who knows me - or has taken this examination - knows how difficult this test is. Roy felt he was up for the task. So, I gave him the lengthy / grueling test and he passed with ease.

In 2006, Roy told me of is desire to test for his black belt in Brazilian Jiu Jitsu - a test that's almost four hours long. He brought a few brutes to his test to demonstrate he was ready.

Early on in the test, one of the brutes cranked really hard on his neck during the headlock escapes portion and Roy had to finish the other 3 hours of the examination with a very sore neck. Trust me when I say I felt his pain!

Then, at the very end of the exam, he had to spar with me and leave everything on the mat. He fought through the pressure of the Boa and became victorious over the war of attrition on his mind, body and emotions.

Mr. Dean was now ready to wear the coveted black belt in Brazilian Jiu Jitsu! He had passed the examination and was not only ready to wear the black belt, but to do so with honor and distinction.

Since taking his first black belt exam, Mr. Dean has blossomed into not only a highly skilled instructor and practitioner, but he has also developed his own method, personality and brand. I am proud of his work!

As of his writing, Mr. Dean has accomplished a ton of very positive goals in his Jiu Jitsu career. In the years to come, I expect him to accomplish even more!

Mr. Dean, you have made your instructor proud! Keep doing what you've been doing. You're on the right path! All the best to you, and the students who are fortunate to call you their instructor!

Sincerely,

Roy Harris,

CEO Harris International

www.RoyHarris.com

CHAPTER 1

THE BOTTOM OF MY SOUL

KENNIN

FORTITUDE

THE BOTTOM OF MY SOUL

A moan just came from the bottom of my soul.

I was in agony.

Air couldn't enter my lungs.

I couldn't move.

But neither could I quit.

I was being crushed alive by a man. Not just any man, mind you. A man who had earned the nickname of "Boa," as in boa constrictor, for his spine twisting, rib breaking, soul-crushingly tight application of Brazilian Jiu Jitsu (BJJ).

This man was one of the famous "Dirty Dozen"; the first twelve Americans to earn their black belt in this powerful art after it leapt to worldwide prominence in the wake of Royce Gracie's display of jiu jitsu in the Ultimate Fighting Championship (UFC).

This man, Mr. Roy Harris, was my instructor, mentor, and friend. In this moment, though, he was hurting me. Smashing me. Effortlessly, I might add, using the weight of his body in a clinical and controlled manner.

Mr. Harris allowed brief moments of mercy where I gasped for air, before he shut down those opportunities at will, eliminating the space that my lungs needed to open. No expansion, just compression. His body on mine, dominating me.

Then a moment of relief.

I struggled to survive, attempting to counter these positions, but Mr. Harris would counter my counter. He was a third-degree black belt, and I was child's play.

Outgunned and outwitted, it became a physical and mental battle in which you're continually losing, yet you cannot quit. You're not expected to win, but you have to keep going.

Even if you're tired, or injured, or don't feel like you have another big movement in you to relieve the relentless pressure, you can't stop.

That's when you begin to moan. Involuntarily. That's when you really dig deep, even though you thought you we're digging deep an hour ago.

You read that right. An hour ago. The test is three and a half hours long, and the moaning is a stunning finale.

That's what this man wants to see. How you react when you're feeling low. Oppressed. When the strength has gone.

Now he can see your true technique. Now he can see your heart. It's not easily exposed. It takes time to get to it. But he'll find it. He knows many ways to get there.

This was a baptism by fire, and the mats of the Harris Academy were the crucible. It was also a launch pad into the realm of leadership, into a realm of mastery that few will ever achieve.

Every birth is a difficult passage, and this was no exception. The tip of my pinky hung like a chad, and was taped to the next finger. The tendon had popped off the bone.

My right ankle was heavily taped and nearly immobilized, football style, since the tendons been snapped in a figure-four toehold six weeks before.

It was only pain, and none of it mattered. Because this was happening. I was getting my black belt, and I was going to finish this test.

You probably already know this, but in case someone hasn't taken the time to point it out, let me do so now.

There's a warrior inside of you. There are a handful of moments in this life where that warrior is pushed to the edge, a distance much farther than you'd ever go by choice. This is where you really learn what you're capable of, and discover who you are, dictated by the demands of the situation.

That willingness to go out on your shield is the very drive that enhances the rest of your life, that allows you to truly live. It's called courage, and it can be tested for extended periods of time, as this ritual was successfully doing.

What this rite of passage did was create a confidence in me, that I could handle anything.

There would be setbacks, of course. Challenges. Injuries. Situations to handle. Risks to take. Yet I knew I could persevere. Because of this moment. Because of this threshold I had crossed.

A black belt from Roy Harris was a lifetime achievement, the culmination of 15 years of continuous training. Starting in Japan, and finishing that afternoon on the mat in San Diego, I was reborn a black belt in Brazilian Jiu Jitsu.

Turn the pages and I'll show you the path. Each step of this process. The real training. The inside scoop. The price of admission, with your body and soul, to achieve nothing more than a piece of cloth.

Why? We thrive on symbols, and that black belt is a symbol of power. A sign of lethal potential. A beacon of physical mastery and emotional calm.

Whatever your projection happens to be, the path to achieving this goal is not what you think. It's not just as you imagined. It's much more intense. It's much more involved.

So let me share one seeker's story, then you'll know if you'd like to take those steps, cross the threshold, and become a black belt yourself.

CHAPTER 2
INTRODUCTION TO THE ART

JUDO

INTRODUCTION TO THE ART

I just was a kid from Anchorage, Alaska, who wanted to see more of the world.

So I looked into an exchange program and, the next thing I knew, I was in Japan my for junior year of high school.

School administrators encouraged me to do a Japanese art after school. I chose Judo.

This is where I tasted the power of real jujutsu for the first time (also spelled jiu jitsu by an older convention).

I was being thrown around easily by my team captain, a spiky-haired teen named Ichikawa, and there was nothing I could do about. Whatever he was doing, it put me on the ground, repeatedly, and gave me an excellent view of the ceiling. I liked what he was doing, and I wanted to be able to do it too.

I trained hard, competed monthly, passed the kata exam, and received my black belt in Kodokan Judo at age of 17 before returning to the US.

My interest in martial arts continued to grow and, after training in Aikido for several years, I decided to get serious and fulfill a dream of becoming a live-in-student, or uchideshi. The masters I admired had all been through this process, and I felt a calling to make it happen.

It wasn't a common arrangement, but I found a Japanese Jujutsu and Aikido master, named Julio Toribio, to take me in.

I moved to Monterey, California and became his first full-time apprentice. There would be many others after, and I put my heart into establishing a program that gives people an intense sampling of the jujutsu lifestyle. I go into that year in great detail in the book, 'The Martial Apprentice.'

By this time, I had already seen Royce Gracie decimate his competition in the UFC. Royce and I had similar builds and, with my olive complexion, one could say we look alike.

His family's art, Gracie Jiu Jitsu, ignited a martial revolution and was taken as a slap in the face for many traditional martial arts practitioners (TMA) who underestimated the effectiveness of an art that, at it's core, limits your movement options in a graceful and systematic manner.

The Gracie Jiu Jitsu that I saw looked similar to the newaza (ground techniques) of Judo, but with a twist: smoother transitions, less space, and more work from your back, a position called "the guard."

While it looked familiar, authentic teachers in Gracie Jiu Jitsu, or it's more open form of Brazilian Jiu Jitsu, were few and far between.

I was living in Seibukan Dojo when a student there mentioned that she had trained in Brazilian Jiu Jitsu before. Her teacher was a Brazilian champion, and she swore up and down that he tapped everyone he rolled with, regardless of their size.

His name was Claudio Franca, and she had an enormous amount of respect for him. She had been injured training at the BJJ school, however. She was dropped on her head during an armbar attempt on a larger male with a far more fragile ego (this is not uncommon, unfortunately). Her neck still wasn't 100%, but she was able to train beside me in Seibukan Jujutsu, rather than its Brazilian cousin.

In time, she made the introduction to her teacher, Professor Claudio Franca and, with the permission of my teacher, I began cross training in BJJ. I could only do it on Friday nights, but I figured that one night a week was better than nothing at all.

Martial arts were my life. This is what I did. I was already living in a dojo, training in every class, every day. What's one more class on top of it?

Claudio's school was in Santa Cruz and I lived 45 minutes away in Monterey, with no car. So I would ride up with my new friend Carolynn, and we began training, then dating.

Claudio's first location was cozy, which was ideal because only the fittest could make it through the warm ups. Calisthenics kicked off every class, then a few techniques were shown, and then some very serious, uncompassionate sparring finished it off.

I can confidently say it was rougher in those days. Guys that would go directly into MMA were now heading over to BJJ to kick ass ASAP, because that's what they saw was working. And people love what's working. They love a winner. And they'll turn on that winner the minute they lose. Such is life.

Given the entry-level skills of the class, effectiveness was more valued than the art's subtle nature. Many of those early sparring sessions felt like they were more about dominance than technique. Guys would even resist you when drilling. We were diamonds in the rough. But whenever I got to see Claudio move, I would be inspired again by how solid, agile, and balanced he was.

There was no YouTube, competition footage was scarce, and only a few VHS instructional sets were on the market, all of which were unaffordable to me. My options were limited, so I gobbled up every piece of information I came across. I was so earnest and hungry for knowledge that I was able to cast the fear of my beatings aside.

I recall tying my white belt in the dressing room before class and feeling my heart beat out of my chest. I was having a low grade panic attack before I stepped on the mat because I knew what was waiting for me: hundreds of pushups, sit-ups and squats, then round after round of full-force, full-contact sparring. While some would call that abuse, I called it Friday night.

Here I was, a black belt in several other martial arts, getting my ass handed to me, and I was OK with it, because I really wanted that knowledge. I was paying my dues. Everyone does if they practice this art.

After 15 months of apprenticeship as a live in student at Seibukan Dojo, I moved out and attended a junior college nearby. I continued to train in both Japanese and Brazilian Jiu Jitsu, and I was quite proud of my latest tribal affiliation.

Claudio had a black sweatshirt that I repped relentlessly around my school. I wanted everyone to know that I was not only a martial artist, but that I did Brazilian Jiu Jitsu, which is what "tough guys" did. Some people actually didn't know that, and they needed to be educated. That's what I was there for. With my black sweatshirt.

No one reps harder than a white belt. No one.

Becoming Blue

I'll never forget the glorious day I got my blue belt. Claudio called me into the office of his Santa Cruz academy. Seated behind his desk, with Garth Taylor at his side, Claudio announced that he was promoting me to the first rank on the path.

I beamed. Finally, I was in "the club." I had earned my admission. White belt days were rough. Words can't do justice to how many beat downs were required for that belt. Suffering had taken place. A lot of heart had been shown.

Yes, it's the first belt. But it MEANT something. At least, to me it did. It was a symbol indicating that I had skill, and someone whom I admired had acknowledged that skill. Previous experience in other arts didn't earn that belt for me, although the movements and coordination helped, of course.

It was persistence that earned that belt. Determination. Checking my ego. And a lot of tapping. This was difficult training on every level. It toughened my spirit and hardened the body. I truly felt like a warrior. A twenty-two year old warrior that healed at a rate I can only marvel at today.

I went to class after class, expecting to receive this hard-earned, heavily coveted, previously announced belt, but left disappointed, time after time.

My impatient self waited a month before Claudio called me to the head of the class, announced that I was a black belt in Japanese Jujutsu, and had now become a blue belt in Brazilian Jiu Jitsu. He tied the belt around my waist and I knew I had crossed a threshold. My first check-point with open road ahead. Amazing!

Things change once you get that belt. Recipients may notice a sharp shift in sparring intensity. It's now open season. That symbol of progress pushes your peers to explore their own position in the hierarchy of skill, especially the white belts. You've reached the standard they wish to achieve, and have become the perfect measuring stick for their own progress. This is your first taste of defending the belt.

Many white belts long for the recognition of promotion, yet forget that they are in the enviable position of having little to no expectations placed on them. At blue, more was expected.

This is what I wanted, right?

It was exactly what I wanted. Heavy is the head that wears the crown. Even though the crown is more like a tiara at blue belt. The crown comes at black belt. Defend the tiara, then we'll talk.

I could defend my belt, but it wasn't clear what the path to purple would look like. I had to train hard, of course. But there was no real curriculum in place, which made things kind of murky.

Then there was competition. Claudio's academy stressed competition, and Claudio himself was a Brazilian and a Pan American champion. I decided to head down that road, not because I longed for head to head conflict, but because I knew it would help my game, and ultimately make my jiu jitsu more effective.

Joe Moreira Invitational

I competed as a blue belt many times. Not all ventures were successful. My first attempt was a Joe Moreira tournament in LA. I drove down from Monterey to Los Angeles with two teammates, Luke and Stan, in my terribly undersized, white Geo Metro.

Stan was a corrections officer with a history in bodybuilding. Luke was a high school wrestler and still growing, but in terms of having space for all of us, it was not the right vehicle.

We were jiu jitsu players traveling on the cheap, leading a life of discomfort, and somehow getting off on it. In L.A., Luke and I shared the bed of a low-end motel and Stan slept on the floor.

You can't imagine how nervous I was about my upcoming match. I had been nervous the entire month leading up to it. I hardly slept at all the night before. Any mental conjuring of what was going to happen in the match would shoot adrenaline through my body, and I had to wait for my rush to ebb out before dropping back to sleep. I knew I needed rest, but my monkey-mind was racing. I was not in full control.

Sun up and it's game day. Even though I wasn't hungry, I choked down some oatmeal and was still on-weight at 173 pounds. We drove to the Irvine Events Center, a beautiful and spacious venue. I matched up with a huge guy from John Lewis' school in Las Vegas.

Was he in the right weight class? Or did he just stumble into my division? Something seemed off.

I walked out onto the mat first. I did a few foot sweeps across the floor, and created the feeling of a Judo practice. My first training. It had been years since I had competed in that art.

When the match began, we tied up, and channeling my Judo roots, I threw him with an uchimata (inner thigh throw). On the ground, he reversed me, passed my guard and kept me in side control. I was trapped. I struggled with every ounce of my being, but failed to escape. Eventually, the realization came that the one or two tricks I had in my bag were simply not enough. Not this time at least.

Looking up from the ground, trapped in side control, the venue seemed larger than life. The ceiling lights felt miles away, like the victory I wanted, but simply could not earn. My opponent won on points as the match came to a close.

I was exhausted. Claudio shook my hand and knew I had given it my all. I was young. A fresh blue. Yes, I had lost, but I had also learned. I had holes in my game that needed fixing. Little did I know that this would always be the case.

This is what competition does. It exposes the weaknesses in your game, rather cruelly, but that's often exactly what you need. It only seems cruel to you. Not to the other guy. He feels like he earned it. Duality can be rough.

Looking back on it now, and comparing it with other competition experiences, I lost the match before I'd even stepped on the mat. How?

Too much energy had been burned in the anticipation of the performance. I didn't have control over my emotions. I didn't even have enough game to finish in the way I thought I could, or had imagined myself doing.

Based on this event, I knew I had a lot of work to do. I continued to train.

The Agony of Defeat

For my next competition, I entered Claudio's very own tournament, the US Open in Santa Cruz, California. In the first round, I matched against Derek DiManno, a student of World Champion and well respected instructor, Cassio Werneck.

As soon as the match began, Derek shot for a single leg takedown. I sprawled and blocked him. He reshot, and raised my leg high. This was the moment that I had been waiting for. This was my moment to shine.

I imagined I was Russian sambo champion, Oleg Taktarov, and dove into a rolling knee bar off of Derek's single leg attempt, inverting myself in the air. Never mind that knee bars weren't allowed at the blue belt level. This was something that I had seen in my mind, a technique that I wanted to use in the competition, so I could get the win in a glorious way. I had daydreamed for months about how cool it would be to win like this.

This was pure martial vanity, and it was about to blow up in my face.

Derek sensed my movement as I dove underneath him and he sprawled out, landing with our bodyweight on the back of my neck.

CRAAAACK! Everything popped. All of it. Every bit of my neck. It was bad. I heard a collective moan from the audience, which is never a good sign. My eyes were closed, but on impact, a flash lit up from my central nervous system. Concussed and coming-to, I attempted to regain guard. Derek fell back for an ankle lock and put me out of my misery.

My neck was seriously jacked up after that match. The more I reflected on it, the more I realized that I could have been paralyzed in that moment. Thankfully I was spared and only suffered from tremendous pain. Walking up the stairs at my junior college, I couldn't stop lightening from surging through my leg and back with every agonizing step.

After a few days of this, and without adequate means, I went to a chiropractor. He was a good friend, an excellent practitioner, and he was nice enough to not charge me. But after two visits I was still in pain. Something else needed to happen, whatever the cost.

I checked in with legendary Monterey chiropractor, Dr. Ed Jarvis. At his office, I took off my shirt and laid facedown on the table. He looked at my spine and said reassuringly "I see what's going on here."

Placing his hands between my shoulder blades, he plunged his weight through his palms and gave me the most satisfying adjustment in the history of vertebrates on this planet.

One crack and my pain went away. Just like that. He adjusted my neck and I was good to go. Healed.

I was so grateful to that man. I still am.

Not all things are equal in this life. There's always a spectrum of skill within the discipline itself. There are doctors that get through the day, and then there are healers.

Ed was a healer. His modality happened to be chiropractic medicine. He could use his skills effectively. It's not just the art. It's also the artist.

I did heal, but I took a break from competing. I continued to train in BJJ, but focused more intently on my sandan (third degree black belt) in Seibukan Jujutsu, and in completing my shodan (first degree black belt) in Aikido under Sensei Toribio.

I loved Sensei's application of Aikido. Smooth, elegant, and backed up by real power. I was determined to become his first black belt in Morihei Ueshiba's art of peace. Then I'd move to San Diego to finish school, and take a well-deserved break from training.

Maybe for a few years, maybe forever. I honestly didn't know. School was the new priority, and martial arts had taken a backseat.

CHAPTER 3
WELCOME TO SAN DIEGO

歓
迎

WELCOME TO SAN DIEGO

I was grateful to be accepted into the University of California, San Diego (UCSD), and I moved from Monterey to begin my studies.

I was hoping to become one of the first graduates of a new, cutting edge program. The ICAM degree (Interdisciplinary Computing and the Arts Major) combined computer science with the fine arts, and had only fielded a few graduates the year before.

Within the program, you could specialize in visual arts or audio engineering. I chose audio, and looked forward to learning the process of writing and recording music digitally.

Junior college was engaging, but not that demanding. UCSD was a different level. Highly competitive. Tough classes. Everybody was smart. Everyone was Asian.

UCSD forced you to teach yourself. Most professors were much better researchers than educators. Students learned in spite of their teachers. They certainly knew what they were talking about, but almost never expressed it in an entertaining and digestible format. This is also common in martial arts.

No spoon-feeding here. Students foraged for themselves, or died in an academic wilderness. So I adapted, and learned the art of self-education. Google became my friend, even though he was the new kid on the block, with only minimalist styling to set him apart from the other search engines of the era.

San Diego was amazing for someone who had grown up in Anchorage. Alaska has a majesty all it's own, don't get me wrong, but this was a living, breathing version of 90210. Kids on skateboards, surf culture and the beautiful SoCal coeds. This is what I had seen on TV. This is what I was walking around in. This was my paradise.

With three million people, San Diego was a huge city to me. The best weather in the world. Beaches, music, and lots of BJJ. There was an energy to Southern California that I connected with. I was twenty-five and it felt like home. Goodbye cold weather. I will not miss you. Not even a little.

I made a very solemn decision not to train in any form of martial arts, so I could fully focus on academics. School was more important that jiu jitsu, even though the latter was clearly more fun. I knew I'd have a heavy workload, and that my performance would have a direct effect on my career success.

I wanted a job when I graduated. No, I needed a job when I graduated. I wanted to be successful. Martial arts would have to go on the back burner. For now. So I limited myself to lifting weights and doing adult gymnastics.

Gymnastics was fascinating. Though I was only involved with it for a short period of time, I saw there was tremendous value in their techniques and training methods. Cross training could yield surprising insights, in unexpected ways. My Judo and Aikido background had already shown me that.

Gymnastics emphasized using your frame, your skeletal structure, rather than relying on muscle to support you. Extend fully. Align properly. This was an epiphany. It redefined the term "posture" in BJJ.

On the first day of gymnastics class, I was told that my limiting factors in performance were going to be strength and flexibility. This is a stunning contrast to the "strength doesn't matter" mantra often recited in martial arts studios.

Gymnastics started with skill development as a warm up, and ended with physical conditioning. It was structured in a progression. Finely tuned movements were executed first, heading towards total exhaustion. You weren't looked on as 'fresh meat' by the more experienced gymnasts. No backflips on the first day, but I still wanted to learn how to properly do a cartwheel guard pass.

Even though I had cross-trained before, the time I spent in gymnastics quickly showed me that other disciplines could strengthen my main art. I filed that information away, and focused on my schoolwork.

A New Teacher

If I hadn't moved to San Diego, I would have stayed loyal to Claudio for the rest of my career. That's just how I am. If I had received a brown belt under him after 7 or 8 years of training, that could have been a real possibility.

But as a blue belt, the expectation is to find a new teacher. You should deeply absorb another lineage and technical influence, but always with appreciation to your first instructor who guided you to that point.

Claudio had introduced me to Fabio Santos at a tournament, telling him I'd be moving down to San Diego, and encouraging me to train at his academy.

I had a tremendous amount of respect for Professor Santos. He could mix it up on the mat, was an inspirational competitor, and was also a fair and attentive referee, which, I feel, reveals a lot about who you are as a teacher.

I've found that one of the best aspects of moving to a new city is the opportunity to look at different martial arts academies, and pick the right fit for me.

The process should be savored. Taken in slowly. Like a fine meal. Examine, ruminate, participate. Although I wasn't allowing myself to train, I wanted to know where I was going to end up if I decided to return. If that ever happened. I wasn't sure yet.

The first stop was Fabio's Academy. It looked good. Full mats. The blue belts appeared uniformly skilled, and there were plenty of them. Vitor Belfort was also opening a school in Pacific Beach, so I checked it out, but missed meeting the man himself. I also went to the Lion's Den, where the ego was so thick you could choke on it. And if you did choke, you weren't allowed to tap.

But it was Roy Harris that intrigued me the most. I had heard about him first from Garth, when I asked about San Diego BJJ options. He described him as having a more "intellectual" approach, probably stemming from his Jeet Kun Do (JKD) background.

He certainly had a buzz going online, and his students seemed to be very loyal. I contacted Michael Jen, who had been a student and training partner of Mr. Harris' for years and, in a lengthy phone conversation, he communicated that Mr. Harris was a teacher who could outline a clear path, and take me to where I wanted to go: black belt.

But I'd settle for purple in the meantime. Or even a single victory in a tournament.

But then again, I wasn't even supposed to be training.

Barona Submission Challenge

In early December, I was on The Underground, an online martial arts forum, when I discovered an upcoming submission tournament at a local casino. Ken Shamrock and the Lions Den would be there, plus a variety of local BJJ schools would be representing. A competition like that is a rock concert for me. I couldn't wait to go.

It was a long drive for the Geo Metro, but I made it to the Indian reservation where the Barona Casino was located. I took a seat in the bleachers.

I was sitting next to several of Odie Neto's students. Odie was a brown belt with his own academy and he was matched in a super-fight with Eddie Millis of The Shark Tank. Unfortunately, Eddie had suffered a neck injury in training, and withdrew from the match at the 11th hour.

But there were many other up-and-coming fighters on the card that were honing their submission skills, including John Alessio, Vernon 'Tiger' White, and Dean Lister.

The main event of the evening was saved as a Ken Shamrock student, Tony Galindo. stepped in to fight Odie. Tony outweighed Odie by at least 20 pounds, and it was all muscle. He was highly conditioned and obviously a fan of the steak and chicken diet.

Despite the Tony's size advantage, Odie used speed and technique to win the match in a masterful display of BJJ. His smooth knee-on-belly transitions allowed him to stay on top at all times. Odie wore him down over several minutes, then took a tight arm lock from knee-on-belly position. Tony resisted but eventually tapped.

Odie's students rushed the mat to lift their leader up. People were hyped about this fight. The BJJ scene in San Diego was smolderingly good. Lots of talent. I knew I was in the right place, the right scene, at the right moment.

The sport needed more events like this one. I approached the announcer, who was also the promoter, Matt Stansell. He was a blue belt under Roy Harris and, if this tournament was a reflection of his teacher, I wanted to know more. Thoughtful match ups, fair refs, and a clean, professional environment.

Matt took a moment to talk to me and, even though it was brief, it felt like a real connection. He admired Mr. Harris and had come to him as a blue belt under Royce Gracie. I knew I had to check this Harris guy out for myself.

Progressive Fighting Systems

I made a promised to myself that there would be no training while at UCSD but, because it was my birthday, I made an exception and attended my first Saturday class at Roy Harris' academy, Progressive Fighting Systems (PFS).

At the time, Mr. Harris was VP of Paul Vunak's PFS association. He created a multi-disciplinary academy, with BJJ being just one of the arts offered. Most of the grappling classes taught were no gi, or without the traditional martial arts uniform, which was well suited to what people actually wore in Southern California.

From the moment I set foot in the school, I loved it. Coming from a classical martial arts background, I found the utter lack of formality refreshing. The common attire was t-shirts and shorts, and some even wore wrestling shoes. I didn't have to bow five times before doing a technique. I could just do the technique. The space had a utilitarian quality that I enjoyed. Nothing fancy. Just real. I was in the right place.

Meeting Mr. Harris for the first time before class, I hurriedly shook his hand and mentioned that I had heard great things about him, and was really looking forward to training.

He looked at me blankly, nodded his head affirmatively and then went into his office. It felt a little cold.

This was a stark contrast to the warmth of many Brazilian instructors, who made you feel like part of their family from the first handshake. But I didn't let it bother me. I wasn't trying to be his best friend. I was there to learn BJJ, and I was looking forward to having him lead me up the mountain of skill and knowledge. I needed help and he could definitely assist me. I knew he could.

I was a solid addition to the PFS BJJ team. Manny Rodrigues was the first guy I rolled with and he double arm locked me from the guard, throwing both legs over my shoulders. Darrin Goo was a purple belt and a silky smooth guard-passing machine. There was talent at this young academy. I had just found a new home.

CHAPTER 4

COMING INTO MY OWN

CONFIDENCE

COMING INTO MY OWN

Kim was a good friend of mine and a dedicated BJJ practitioner under Claudio.

She poured a tremendous amount of her time, energy, and talent into the sport by both competing in and videotaping tournaments.

She also took beautiful photos of jiu jitsu players in action.

A huge supporter of the team, she would occasionally sponsor starving martial artists, such as myself, to test their skills.

Kim was always encouraging me to compete. Sometimes it seemed like she believed in my abilities even more than I believed them myself.

I drove up to LA from San Diego and met up with Kim for another of Joe Moreira's tournaments. This tournament was a little different. It was held in a corner of an African American cultural festival, and the mats were placed over dirt, under a canopy.

A future black belt named Gazzy Parman was registering competitors, and hearing that I was under Roy Harris (she knew him personally), she told me I'd be competing for Joe Moreira that day, which is Mr. Harris' instructor. No problem for me, of course, it's all the family.

I did some special preparation for this tournament at Judo America, run by the progressive coach Gerald LeFon, 7th dan. But all that Judo training didn't help a bit in my first match against Jason Brudvik, a student of Javier Vasquez of Millenia Jiu Jitsu.

As soon as the match started, Jason jumped guard, and my weeks of Judo evaporated. He shot his hips up so fast for submissions, it was unbelievable (I watched another of his matches Kim had recorded and it actually looked like the footage had been sped up. Really impressive).

Although I escaped his first arm lock, I succumbed to a triangle choke shortly after. The submission was so tight that I chipped my tooth.

This was getting old. Another tournament, another match, another loss. I rapped with Jason after the match and he invited me to see his upcoming MMA fight at King of the Cage.

I actually made it to his cage fight that night at Sobaba Casino, and Jason handled his business quickly, winning in the first round by triangle, of course.

Jason had this jiu jitsu thing down.

Clearly, I didn't.

I was sick of losing. It really fucking bothered me. Every match I had undertaken in BJJ had been a loss. Every one. And this is for a guy who trained diligently. Who trained seriously. It was messing with my self-image, and nobody likes that. The image must be maintained. At all times and at all costs.

I had black belts in others arts, plus competition experience in Judo. Here was my chance to test out my submission skills in a full contact, full speed, full power setting. Yes, it's a limited rules fight, as all combat sports are, but the technical palette of BJJ is pretty diverse. No punching or kicking, but throws, slams, chokes, arm locks, and leg locks were all legal.

From an evolutionary standpoint, my DNA would have died with every blue belt match so far. This was depressing information.

I was learning all that I could with the limited resources I had, along with the scarce resources on the market.

I wasn't short on dedication. I wasn't short on heart. Am I not a man? I could see other guys winning, and I began to emulate what they were doing.

Kim videotaped my match and I showed it to Mr. Harris. His advice was simple:

I needed to get more aggressive.

This had been an issue for a long time. I'm a good guy. A "nice" guy. I wanted people to like me and respect my skill. I yearned to have the ability to dominate with minimal energy and perfect technique. I never wanted to roll too hard, for fear of unbridled escalation or, basically, just being a dick.

Sound familiar? I think it's a common issue amongst non-meatheads. I didn't know how to differentiate between being clinically aggressive on the mat without being perceived as rough. I had to find that middle path.

Getting on that path required me to ramp up my aggression at that point in time. I was holding back. I needed to figure out how to win. I needed to change and, although change is rarely comfortable, I was determined to make it happen.

I took a suggestion from Mr. Harris to add another element to my martial studies that made all the difference: a training partner.

Another Brother

I met Brad Hirakawa at a Saturday morning class at PFS. I caught him in a triangle choke, and he tapped me with a knee bar. Seemed like a cool guy. Blue belt. Half Japanese. A scientist working for a small bio-tech company in San Diego, slaying rats for the greater good in a long term bid to cure cancer.

I needed to do something different to break out of these blue belt blues I found myself in. Yes, I had a good triangle choke and a decent sleeve choke, but I bored myself with my game.

I had a couple of tricks. They were effective, but limited, and I had to do something different in my training if I wanted a different result.

Mr. Harris mentioned in one of his articles that a good training partner was worth his weight in gold.

I approached Brad about drilling on a regular basis and he was all in. We began meeting at the Combat Room at UCSD, which was a matted and padded space, usually reserved to teach martial arts. Then the work began.

The drills were simple: foot lock entries, guard passing, arm lock and triangle combinations, and a few throws. As the repetitions increased, week after week, something marvelous happened. The time it took to switch from one technique to another almost disappeared.

We were no longer jumping from technique to technique; we were smoothly stepping to the next spot. We connected with our partner and began working with them, rather than trying to do something to them.

Sensitivity is the ability to read and feel pressure. This process of drilling developed our sensitivity to each other, which would transfer into real skill against any future opponent.

We were in sync, and beginning to own our movements rather than just sketch their shapes. Machine level language was being programmed in that we could build upon.

Soft and firm, yielding and tight, slow and fast. Jiu Jitsu plays with these opposites, and owning the movements allowed you to mix and match the tempos during their application to fit the situation. Most beginners try to create the situation through athleticism and power. It's important to work with what you have, what you're given, rather than looking for something that simply isn't there.

That leap in sensitivity was profound. We were soon finding little gems, hidden ways of increasing efficiency through small movements in every technique. Push with your knee there; place your hand a few inches higher; squeeze in this direction.

There was now a depth to every technique that hadn't been there before. It's as if I was drawing on paper, and the image suddenly became three-dimensional. Things opened up. There was space that I hadn't felt before.

Every technique had neighbors, so our understanding was expanding in both breadth and depth.

Brad and I developed our games together and, eventually, he became as much of a brother as a friend. Mr. Harris' suggestion of getting a training partner turned out to be a life-changing event.

People could see that both of our games had made serious gains. There's something unique and indelibly sweet about feeling the momentum of your progress in BJJ. When it's happening, jiu jitsu is the best thing in the world. It's incredibly motivating and the rewards can come in rapid succession.

During times like these, it can be hard to relate to those that are frustrated or burnt out. Essentially, your life revolves around jiu jitsu. It has to, for a certain period of time, if you really want to get good at it. There are many times when jiu jitsu demands complete dedication.

I endured a multi-year plateau at blue belt, so I appreciated the progress as it happened. I knew it wasn't always like that, and I needed to keep the pedals turning and ride this baby as far as I could take it.

Grapplers Quest 2000

Kim told me about a new no gi tournament happening in Las Vegas called Grappler's Quest. I signed up right away. Even though I had been training in the gi most of my life, I adapted quickly to the no gi grappling environment at PFS.

Kim bought me a ticket to Las Vegas from San Diego and I flew out with a new spring in my step. I was confident I would have a good showing at this tournament. I had nothing to lose, and my jiu jitsu idol, Dan Camarillo, was going to be there. Not to compete, just to watch, and, if I was lucky, possibly coach me during my match.

The venue was Durango High School, and the man checking in the competitors was also the organizer, Brian Cimins.

This was the first time I had ever seen a laptop used for tournament registrations, and was suitably impressed. It was a clear indicator that the sport was growing to another level of professionalism. I had high hopes this event would actually run on time, and I wasn't disappointed.

No gi grappling doesn't generally have belt levels for competitors, they go by years of experience, classifying you as beginner, intermediate, or expert. As a blue belt, I signed up for the intermediate division at middleweight (170 -179 pounds).

Because I registered early, or perhaps simply through random selection, I got a bye in the first round. That meant that I had one less match than my opponents, and automatically advanced to the second round.

I noticed that some of the guys in my division were going to war in long matches. I used that time for a thorough warm up, while noting that you have to be aggressive in competition, even at sign up. It paid off this time.

There was a mantra I kept repeating as I prepared for my match. "This is my time. I will not lose. This is going be my coming out party."

The wording should have probably been different, but it was true in the BJJ sense. This was a new fighter emerging. Highly focused. Sweep the leg. No mercy sir.

It's my turn to step on the mat. My opponent, Abel Moreno, and I hand fight for a bit, then he goes for a wrist lock (kote gaeshi). It's on fairly tight, but by stepping ahead of where he was when he was applying the submission, I was able to straighten out of his hold and free my wrist. I was surprised by the attack.

Wasn't I supposed to be attacking the wrist, as an Aikido black belt? How dare he. As I reached to tie up around his neck with my left arm, Abel swung

BECOMING THE BLACK BELT

into waki gatame, or a standing arm lock, dropping his entire bodyweight on my elbow, and falling to the ground.

This is a very powerful technique that's banned in modern Judo. You can look up Shinya Aoki breaking a man's arm with this move in an MMA match. It's terrible. Hearing the bone break may not be something you forget easily. Fair warning to the curious.

My opponent almost had me in that waki gatame. With my arm fully extended, he dropped to his knees to finish the fight and eliminate any chance of my escape.

This is where my classical training saved me. All those years of ukemi, with the thousands of rolls I had performed, paid off in a split second reversal of fortune.

I somersaulted over my head and rolled out. It wasn't a perfect roll. I clipped my head on the way over, but I didn't have a lot of space or time to work with, so I was happy just to do it. Imperfect, yet effective. Could this be the story of my life?

I rolled to a closed guard position and threw my leg around his head for an arm lock. I thrust my hips hard and the arm bar was already on tight. He picked me up off the ground but I did not relent. I was taking this home with me. I applied continuous pressure to his elbow and he tapped while I was still in the air! My back hit the mat as I released the hold.

I won. My first victory in BJJ. By submission.

I am a man after all.

Whew.

Match Two: I faced a shorter and more muscular competitor. I suspect he came from a wrestling background. I attempted to throw him with uchimata but failed, eventually pulling guard. At one point I hunted for a rolling arm lock from the back but couldn't finish, then he tried to pass but couldn't complete it. Eventually, he retreated and I followed him up to the feet. We hand fought a little and, after another takedown attempt, we spun to the ground where I held him in guard.

By that point in the match I was tired, but I knew that he was tired too. It was a lung burning, oxygen deprived grind, but I embraced it and kept pushing.

He reached back to open my ankles and I slapped on a triangle. He tapped for my second submission victory and the gold medal at the first Grappler's Quest competition was mine.

I was a champion. I could do it. Finally.

Another threshold had been crossed.

The elite invitational tournament was also a who's who in the grappling scene: Dean Lister, Tony DeSouza, Jeff Monson, Garth Taylor, Alexander "Cafe" Dantas, Sean Spangler, Alberto Crane, Homer Moore, JD Penn, Chris Brennan and Marc Laimon.

Brennan and Laimon had a bit of heat between them. They were roommates for a time while they trained at Gracie Torrance, and the Internet had contributed to the hype of their pairing. Laimon reversed a Kimura attempt by Brennan into a straight arm lock and beat him in under a minute, eventually winning the entire division by outpointing Dean Lister in the finals.

BJ Penn also won his super fight against Mike Cardoso, and everyone headed to the official nightclub where we partied as you can only do in Vegas.

As Kim and I headed back to the hotel, we picked up a teammate, Paul Schreiner, who was in need of a place to crash. He slept soundly in the second bed as this incredible day came to a close.

US Open 2001

I had a definite momentum when I returned to San Diego. It was a very cool feeling walking back into the gym, and seeing Matt Stansell give me the nod that said, "Hey, I know what you just did." The hero's homecoming.

The next competition was the US Open in Santa Cruz. I was far more confident now that I knew I could get it done. This time, I wouldn't end up on my neck. No knee bars. Just arm locks and triangle. The stuff that I was actually good at, not what I imagined might look impressive.

The blue belt middleweight division is always tough, and it was definitely the largest of this tournament. Because it was so huge, the organizers scheduled it for the start of the day, rather than the lightest weight class.

My first round opponent was a student of the Machados. I saw him lightly jogging on the mat before the division started, with two hoop earrings and some long sideburns. He looked nervous and a little too well groomed for this crowd.

When the match began, I tried to throw him with an uchimata, of course, but I didn't have it. He grabbed me and worked for a single leg. Rather than fighting it, I sat down and attempted a sacrifice throw. That was also unsuccessful and I worked from guard, while he was awarded two points.

I attempted to sweep him and created enough space to scramble back to my feet. My opponent immediately picked me up with a double leg and slammed me to the mat.

Boom. It was the wake-up call that I needed. The points didn't matter. Slamming me mattered. Now I was in the fight. He stood up from my guard, gripping my pants with his left hand and holding my sleeve with his right, he rotated me into an arm lock, threw his leg over my face and attempted to finish right away.

I felt it coming and, as he sat into the submission, I had already begun my escape. I twisted my arm, nullifying his angle for the arm lock, rolled backwards over my shoulder and then got up on my feet. I immediately passed his guard, secured knee on belly position for points, then sat into the same arm lock I was in only seconds before.

He sat up to escape but I was determined. I straightened his arm and he tapped. We shook hands on our feet, and the referee raised my hand in victory.

I had one or two matches to recover before I was on deck again, this time against a seventeen year old named Nick Diaz from the Cesar Gracie academy.

The match began and Nick immediately pulled guard. My guard passing was decent, so I aggressively attempted an under the leg pass. This pass relied on using the pressure of my sprawled frame and bodyweight to push his legs to the side as I latched on to his upper body.

As I leaned into the sprawl position against his legs, I experienced, for the first time in my life, what athletes call "hitting the wall".

Suddenly, I had no energy. None. The gas tank was empty and there were miles to go. Yes, I have been tired before, but never completely bonked. This wasn't good.

My mind was sending signals, and my body would eventually respond and move forward, but there was a delay. A terrible, terrible delay, in a very immediate situation.

It felt like a two-second lag between the order being issued from my mind and the action being executed by my body, at a moment where milliseconds made all the difference. I went from broadband to dialup in an instant, finding myself immersed in a true battle of wills.

I passed Nick's guard, but didn't establish the proper anchors to his upper body first, before moving to knee on belly position. My hips were too high and, as I slid my shin across his belt line, Nick reversed me with a bridge. Now I was on the bottom, scrambling desperately to regain guard.

Nick moved to north south position, and I defiantly rolled to my knees. He adjusted to a near crucifix, on my back and perpendicular to my body.

I did a wrestling sit out and, as I escaped, I reached up and grabbed Nick's head, sweeping him on to his back. Now I was on top again.

All I wanted to do was rest, but I had to capitalize on being in the top position. I hopped over his leg and passed one more time, but Nick was squirrelly and spun around to put me back in open guard.

He snapped on a triangle, but I rolled my shoulder and slipped out. I continued passing but couldn't get control of that collar to anchor my weight.

That's when Nick reached up from the bottom, locked his hands in a figure four, and secured a Kimura. I was forced to hop three hundred and sixty degrees around his body to counter the position and return to his open guard. That was a close call. He almost had that.

I sprawled heavily against his legs and surfed my way down to side control. Nick made a little bit of space, secured another Kimura, and rolled me over.

Dammit! This kid and his Kimuras. I worked hard to get to that position, and now Nick was on his knees, straddling my head and shoulders and about to finish the bent arm lock. I laid on my side, clutching my belt with my left hand, the last line of defense as he yanked hard to free my arm and secure the submission.

Kim, recording the match on the sidelines, was screaming at me: "Get out! Escape!" I knew what I had to do, so I took my right hand, lifted my first finger, and let her know that I needed a minute. Please. I'll get to it in a second. We're on the same page here.

Jiu jitsu isn't about escaping when you want to, it's about escaping when you can, and the opportunity was just about to present itself.

I could feel that Nick was getting ready to break the hold and secure the shoulder lock, so as he lifted my arm and brought it behind my back, I went with it, rather than fighting the motion, and even adding a little bit to it.

I spun into the submission at the same rate that my arm was moving, which kept it safely in front of my chest, then hopped over his leg in the opposite direction. I rolled to my knees, then into him again, which freed my elbow from the figure four.

I barely escaped that attack, and was more tired than ever.

I rolled to my knees and hooked his thigh for a single leg with both arms. Nick reached down, pulled my ankle towards him, which collapsed me back to guard. He attempted to pass, but I managed to get my shin across his stomach, and swept him on to his back.

I came up on top, after a few moments in side mount, and Nick managed another escape by grabbing the back of my pants for a little extra leverage and bridging hard.

I was crushed. I could feel it happening in slow motion and did NOT want to go over, but I had to. It was the physics of disappointment.

As I struggled to get to my knees, Nick took my back. We spun several times as he attempted to secure the second hook and receive the four points for the position. Eventually, he got that second hook.

Down on points, I felt dejected.

Then, Nick uttered two magic words that gave me new life:

From the top of my head, I heard: "I'm dying."

As soon as that was said, I escaped a back hook and shook him off. I passed his guard by going straight to knee on belly, but he threw his foot on my hip and prevented the points.

Time was up, the match was over, and Nick had won, four to two.

As the referee brought us to the center of the mat to raise his hand, he said to us both, "Beautiful fight, guys. Best fight of the day."

Even if I had managed to get the win, given how exhausted I was, I'm not sure I could have continued to the next round. Claudio later told me that Nick was also feeling the effects, and begged for more recovery time before his next match. Even so, the kid managed to submit the rest of his opponents to capture the gold.

His crew approached me after the match and asked who I was, where I trained, etc. I guess it was rare to see their boy in such a hard fought battle, and Nick and I rapped out for a few minutes with mutual respect.

"Yeah man, you're good. But I must have eaten something at breakfast that messed me up. I felt sick. Seriously. I wasn't myself out there."

I must have eaten the same thing. Regardless, I returned to San Diego with my head held high. Win or lose, this was another valuable experience on the journey. I was making progress, paying my dues and gaining momentum.

I rolled that confidence into the United Gracie tournament in San Francisco, submitting all of my opponents until the finals, where I squared off against Marcos Torregrossa, another Cassio Werneck student. He submitted me with a rather awesome triangle to arm lock combination, leaving me with a sore elbow, a silver medal, and a silver lining:

Marcos had just won the world championship at blue belt. So if was only dropping matches to the best blue belt in the world, that's really not so bad.

I had a feeling my purple belt was just around the corner.

CHAPTER 5
THE HARRIS ACADEMY

DOJO

TRAINING HALL

THE HARRIS ACADEMY

Jiu jitsu is fun. It's enjoyable at white belt and blue belt. Of course. It's fun to learn the art. It's even more enjoyable to perform the art.

Of course, jiu jitsu is a never-ending journey that requires a lifetime of learning, but once you receive your purple belt, you can really focus on improving your performance. Not learning how or what to perform.

In other words, now that you know how to drive, you can focus on the race itself, rather than the mechanics of steering, shifting, and wondering where to turn.

This is when a flow emerges in your BJJ, when the transitional movements between techniques has become smooth. Pivots are tight. Timing is on. Tapping people gets easy, and you begin to feel the power of the art.

You're beating skilled opponents, not just newbies off the street, and your "A game", your most reliable and trusted techniques, come to light. This is the framework you'll build upon for years to come. This is your foundation.

At purple belt, attacking with a technique is not the challenge; it's timing the attack. The technique has become second nature. You improve your timing and learn additional entries so all roads lead where you want them. To the trap. To your strengths. To your best submissions.

It's about going deeper in your current skill set, rather than adding new techniques. Depth, not breadth. Extra baggage can slow you down. There are times to pare down your possessions. It's the same with your techniques. It depends on your stage in the journey.

The Harris Academy had become a second home. Our patriarch, Mr. Roy Harris, is a very unique man. Half African-American, half American-Indian. Adopted by a white family, homeless as a teenager due to a religious conversion which his family couldn't accept, he fell in love with martial arts in Minneapolis and moved to San Diego to pursue his passion.

While training at the Inosanto Academy, one of his friends told him about Gracie Jiu Jitsu. His buddy was selling it as highly effective, but Mr. Harris had his doubts. Harris was very confident in his stand up skills. His buddy offered to prove it, right there, and he did so. Immediately. In the parking lot, on the pavement.

He shot a double leg, took Mr. Harris down and mounted him. Mr. Harris turned over and received a rear naked choke for his efforts. This was repeated, and Mr. Harris understood that there was something real and undeniably effective about this art. He began to explore it for himself.

It began at the Gracie Academy in Torrance, California. His first private lesson was with Royler Gracie and it was even more eye opening to have such a small guy escape, sweep and submit Mr. Harris at will. His respect for the art grew further as he realized it could be executed with a gentle spirit and playful approach, yet still be completely dominant. He received his blue belt after thirteen lessons, as his aptitude for grappling grew.

He went from school to school, parting ways for a variety of reasons. Money issues, sharing techniques with the wrong person, taking a private lesson at another school, etc.

That might seem inconsequential, that it wouldn't even raise an eyebrow. But it was a totally different era back then. Fighting techniques were closely guarded secrets and the BJJ familia was much more like the mafia. It was in group/out group thinking to the max.

He found a home with Joe Moreira. Joe knew jiu jitsu (and judo) very well. He was a crusher who was connected with the prominent BJJ families of the era (the Gracie, the Machados, etc). He listened to their reservations about taking on Mr. Harris as a student, but Joe made his own decision.

As long as you were a good person, and loyal, he didn't care what anyone else said about you. You were his student.

Joe would later cause an uproar for giving Marco Ruas a black belt, as well as Kimo Leopoldo, who faced Royce Gracie in UFC III. Despite the occasional controversial promotion, no one could doubt his knowledge or execution of techniques.

There are stories of him rolling up high level BJJ and MMA fighters in training. He fought a young champion twenty years his junior and broke the poor man's rib on a guard pass, winning the match. The man knows his craft, and he's produced many great black belts.

Mr. Harris is arguably one of his best. Promoted to the rank in 1999, Mr. Harris became one of the Dirty Dozen, one of the first twelve Americans to earn their black belt in the art of Brazilian Jiu Jitsu.

Although Joe put him through a test that included a multiple attacker, anything-goes-scenario, Mr. Harris' true initiation came a few weeks after his promotion. He faced the legendary Jean Jacques Machado in the Joe Moreira Black Belt Challenge, as the final fight of the evening.

Here's the backstory:

Years earlier, when Mr. Harris was training at the Machado Academy, he caught Rigan in an exotic submission known as a banana split. Apparently Rigan was cool about it, but Jean Jacques was not. He rolled next with Mr. Harris and administered a beat down for all to see.

People in the crowd that evening thought a similar event might happen; a total destruction of Mr. Harris by the great Jean Jacques. But it didn't go down like that.

Instead, it was an intense back and forth match, with Jean Jacque getting several sweeps and passing his guard. Mr. Harris reversed him to the gasp of the crowd, and had the only near submission of the match (a Kimura which he transitioned to a straight armlock). Mr. Harris continued his offense until the end, where Jean Jacque protected himself to maintain his lead and wisely avoided a last minute leg lock. Though he lost on points, Mr. Harris earned enormous respect that evening for his fighting spirit and technical display.

One of the audience members impressed with his match was Howard Liu of Howard Combat Kimonos (HCK), a company renown for their world class grappling gear. Mr. Liu was actually a Machado student and, in time, would sponsor both Mr. Harris and myself.

As an instructor, Mr. Harris is second to none. I've been fortunate to have excellent teachers throughout my entire martial arts career, but Mr. Harris is in a very special category: an instructor's instructor.

If you're looking for a father figure, or a coach that will tell you exactly when to eat and how many miles to run, you've found the wrong man. But if you're looking for the twenty-one details of the triangle choke, or the seven major and minor grips with the gi, you've found the right guy. There is a curiosity which encourages him to deeply explore answers to the questions of "Why" or "What", far beyond most mortal men.

Mr. Harris once did a thought experiment where he wrote down areas to train in grappling. He penned exactly five thousand, one hundred and fourteen before stopping. He remembers the number. He's a little bit Superman, a little bit Spock. But truly a moral and honest individual if I've ever met one.

He cares about his students, as people as well as martial artists. He had counseled many people, not just students, through difficult times, and done a tremendous amount of good for the community around him.

As a devout Christian, he believes in good and evil, and that there's something greater than us. Something even greater than, gasp, the competition jiu jitsu scene. He has the right kind of perspective on what it is that he teaches, and how martial arts is a hobby to 98% of practitioners. He is a giver, and he never sold out to hop on the money train.

I know there was an art that was shown to him privately, which his instructor asked him to not teach publicly. So he didn't, even though there was ample opportunity to capitalize on it.

Honor, loyalty, and integrity. He understands what these terms mean.

His ground game is off the charts. He's put in the time on the mats, not just here, but all around the world, grappling people from varied backgrounds and disciplines. He's had special forces members attack him by surprise, grabbing his testicles and gouging his eyes, and still come out on top. He's got the self-defense thing worked out, on top of his BJJ skills.

His pressure in the ground game, like his teacher, has broken ribs on occasion. He's also known for his foot lock expertise and incredibly detailed instruction. In all the years I've rolled with him, I've never tapped him out. He's let me do it, of course, but I know I've never really earned it.

To be honest, I've never seen him dominated on the mat. That's not to say it couldn't happen, but in the years I trained with him, he could represent the art masterfully.

Back in the day, there was a little bit of static between Fabio Santos and Roy Harris in the SoCal scene. Fabio was irritated that Roy had opened up shop in San Diego and was encroaching on his territory, there had also been some talk from those quarters that Harris wasn't very good.

Every man has his limit, and Mr. Harris eventually reached a point where he was fed up with hearing the trash talk. He went to Professor Santos' academy and politely participated in a private lesson. He thanked him for the training, made peace, and never went back.

No more talk after that. Respect had been earned.

As tough and skilled as he is, every Superman has his Kryptonite. A large spider once scurried across the mat of the Harris Academy and Mr. Harris jumped five feet back, grabbed a Kali stick, and ran up some stairs to maintain distance. Al Lowrimore, tough guy extraordinaire, let the spider crawl onto his hand and gently placed it back outside.

No man is invincible, but beating Mr. Harris would probably involve eight hairy legs and a couple of fangs. At least it would be a good start.

Giving Back

I received my purple belt from Mr. Harris in a private lesson. We did some training, he felt my game, and at the end of the hour, he shook my hand and said, "You can now wear the purple."

There was a recognized transmission of knowledge. That belt had been earned over many years, and I was ecstatic.

I drove to the Gala house and as I approached, Brad was already standing in the entrance. I opened the screen door and instantly gave him a huge bro hug. "I got it." I said, and Brad beamed. He was just as stoked as I was.

I wouldn't have been able to go to that next level, in that time frame, without having him as a training partner. Shortly after, Brad received his purple belt as well.

Without consciously knowing it, we were entering a golden era in our lives. One we would both look back on fondly, with a slight sense of wonder at how smoothly everything worked out.

Giving back began at purple belt. Brad and I each took a night teaching at the Harris Academy. We also took over the UCSD BJJ public recreation class for Mr. Harris, who had led it for over a decade.

Mr. Harris was very busy, doing seminars around the world, putting in hour after hour on the road to create an international network of instructors. We were always happy to see him and help out when he returned home.

The USCD class was a highly anticipated and somewhat predictable experience.

It always started out with huge numbers. Forty plus students would be on the roster at the beginning of the quarter. Lots of energy in the room. Guys jogging in place and warming up in the corners. It was mostly students, but there were also off-campus adults joining in. A few women too, but mainly men.

Classes were no gi, with simple and to the point instruction. Sparring would begin the first day. This often resulted in people going for it like a life and death struggle, though we constantly encouraged them to relax, go slow, and have fun.

Surprisingly, there were very few injuries, but the intensity of sparring with full resistance from the first day caused many people to drop out over the quarter. Not what they thought, too damn hard, or just too busy with the demands of academics.

What we were left with was a small group of hardcore students who couldn't get enough of this BJJ thing, and many of those survivors found their way into the Harris Academy.

Brad and I loved the experience. We were delving deeper into the BJJ lifestyle, and not just training, but also sharing what we practiced so diligently and intently: the art of defeating capable men in unarmed combat.

Around this time, I turned Brad onto a fitness methodology called Crossfit. Founder Greg Glassman had operated out of Claudio Franca's academy in Santa Cruz, training both Claudio and Garth, who was one of the first to ever sport Crossfit patches on his gi during competitions.

At the time, Crossfit was just starting to attract interest from high-end athletes like Olympian Eva Twardokens, and those with scientific backgrounds, such as biochemist Robb Wolf. Brad fit perfectly into both categories: the athlete scientist, who became Crossfit's first muscle up "king" in addition to contributing his scientific knowledge to the burgeoning online community.

Brad and I were still living in the Gala house in a quiet residential area, with a third roommate named Craig. Brad and Craig worked together, and they had also been roommates at their Pacific Beach pad before adding me to the mix.

Our Crossfit gym was in the fully matted, open patio are behind the house. Matted from wall to wall, it was a huge athletic canvas. We trained all the time. It was a big part of our day. We would drill arm locks and throw in a set of squats. Couple that with the warm weather of San Diego and we were definitely in some kind of martial paradise.

Sometimes we'd roll at night, or have parties where training was an option. Gi's hung next to the sliding glass door. That house had magic to it. We were living the life, and it had nothing to do with material success. It was the joy of living with purpose, and training with proper intent.

CHAPTER 6

SONGS AND PROFESSIONS

SONGS AND PROFESSIONS

UCSD stretched me. It expanded my own perception of what I was capable of.

The goal within this new major was to create a generation of digital artists, capable of creating their own tools.

If I had attended a recording school like Full Sail or even the Music Technology program at the Berkeley School of Music, I would have gotten good at recording voices and instruments on a variety of equipment. I would have been learning the basics, doing work, and mimicking sessions as they'd go down in the real world.

That was the kind of experience I overtly craved, because I knew it would give me greater confidence when applying for positions outside of academia.

It seemed like UCSD wanted to keep you away from all matters practical. The idea in the program was to give students the ability to create their own tools, their own instruments, and build the interfaces of tomorrow.

That's what the programming requirements were for, whether it was Java, or building a drum machine from scratch.

I discovered something about myself during this process. We are all programmers in one way or another, and it's important to identify the level of programming that you perform best at.

For example, machine code is the root level, then the particular computer language (Swift, PHP, Java, Fortran, Visual Basic) builds on top of it, then the program itself. Some people program with programs, in a movie for example, generating content from multiple software applications to create a single piece of art.

MIDI (Musical Instrument Digital Interface) programming is, what I found, I was best suited to, using a program called Cubase. I was good at taking a single tool and creating something interesting, and occasionally clever, with it. That was my strength, not the building of the tool itself, one level down. Steve Jobs, while not being a coder, edited and arranged the lines of his company to create a triumphant score for art, culture, and technology with Apple. Few can conduct a commercial enterprise so masterfully, yet it's what he was best at. You have to find your level.

I found a mentor in Professor Peter Otto (P.O.), the Chief Technology Officer in the UCSD Music Department. Just like martial arts, there is a lineage in electronic music. Peter's mentor was a man named Morton Subotnik, and his teacher was the grandfather of electronic music, Karl Stockhausen.

P.O. had listened to a tremendous amount of music over the years: classical, modern, avant garde and more. Aurally literate to the max, his ability to find just the right words to describe the shades, tones, and textures of music was uncanny and always inspiring.

I would occasionally show up at his office panicked, deeply concerned with being able to get a job after graduation. I knew the wretched fate of many music majors, including those with masters and PhD's, vying for a handful of jobs.

The first graduate from the ICAM program was Kent Oberlin, who was hired right away by Sony Pictures. He got a killer job, and I wanted to follow in his footsteps.

If I had unlimited resources, or was a trustafarian, I could have gone to graduate school or even the film score program at USC (University of Southern California, although many contest it actually means University of Spoiled Children). This would have served the dual purpose of furthering my education and avoiding the real world for another two to three years.

But that was not my fate. I was already borrowing money to get through school, and I needed a real plan in place to get a real job. There are the haves and the have-nots in the world, and I was determined to be a have. I was willing to do the work, I just needed the right direction.

Peter's advice to me was clear: learn ProTools, and you'll have a job.

ProTools, by Digidesign, had become the de facto industry standard for hard drive recording on a Digital Audio Workstation (DAW). At that time, ProTools had both a hardware and a software component to it, and it was prohibitively expensive. ProTools was only available in the university's music studio, B111, and time in that room was meticulously scheduled.

There was a small scale, limited feature, not for public release version of Pro-Tools that Peter had been sent, which apparently worked natively without the external hardware component.

I tried to install it on my computer, but it was a no go. But the thought itself was intoxicating. A version of ProTools you can have on your laptop! Editing audio with a pair of headphones anywhere! The future looked bright.

I was finally able to take the cool classes I had been waiting for since my junior year. The studio class led by Peter was a game changer. Academic audio geeks would gather in room B 111, listen, and share their latest creations.

The class gave me a long awaited opportunity to work with ProTools, as well as an analog mixing board, voiceover booth, and a bunch of other gear in a state of the art studio. Peter gave us assignments, and we would play our midterm and final projects for the class.

The midterm assignment was a two-minute audio composition and, although I didn't know ProTools, I knew the kind of materials I wanted to import to manipulate in the medium. There were a few tracks from my CD collection I'd wanted to sample for several years and, now that I had a chance, I was taking it.

I didn't overthink my mini composition. I just took the best material, compiled it into several audio tracks and "bounced" the final result. That bounced (exported) file could then be burned onto an actual CD, which could be played in any CD player! How awesome was that?

The midterm audio review was soon upon us and, based on the compositions I'd heard, there were some talented people in the room. Not all efforts were entirely coherent, but all were passable.

It was my turn to play my track. Many of the students knew each other. Some were even repeating the class and improving their skills. I was the new guy, and a little nervous to hit play and have my thoughts emanate through the speakers.

The track opened with a man shouting in German, lifted from Arnold Schoenberg's 'A Survivor from Warsaw'. Behind the officer shouting at the Jews was an Yngwie Malmsteen guitar lick, a rough and heavy wah-wah rhythm lifted from his Moscow concert.

That cacophonous scene came crashing to a halt and dropped the listener into an alternate universe of ephemeral strings and ghostly female voices. "No, I'm very, very shy" was a sexy sample from Steve Vai's 'Passion and Warfare' album, stretched and manipulated to great effect.

Metallic emanations gained from spectral abstraction shot past the listeners' ears as Jewel's voice slowly seeped into the speakers, cooing "I'm your Angel" in the final sample, and providing an effortless and coherent escape to end the piece.

The track finished. Students murmured. Peter and the TA looked at each other and exchanged some kind of non-verbal communication that I wasn't sure how to place.

Then Peter said, "Play it again."

I did. At the end, I realized that I had just hit a home run off my first time at bat.

Little did I know that it would never be that easy again.

"What was that sample?" They asked. "How did you get that sound?"

Wow. I explained it all. This was a good sign. In fact, this might be the future. People patted me on the back. The new kid just did it.

Side note: I was never able to impress him to the same degree I did that day. Believe me, I tried.

People were anxious to hear what I was going to do the next. I was sure that it would be a heartbreaking work of staggering genius. Except that it wasn't. When I hit play in ProTools at the end of the quarter, it was applauded, but not the home run I had on my first attempt.

When I asked him what the difference was, the P.O. came through in a big way. He shared something that continues to influence me to this day.

"Roy, think of your first song as a room. When you're building a house, it needs to be laid out in a specific way. A house isn't just a big room."

He was so right. So fucking right. My material, although I had added to it and expanded on it, had been stretched too thinly over the course of 5 minutes. I had built an XL room, not a house, not a home, and it was definitely not as compelling.

I winged it and went with my intuition, but I would have been better off learning a classic form and imitating it. Learn the rules, then break them. Learn them in order to break them.

I repeated the Studio course in my senior year, partnering with classmate Jeff Johnson, who played a little guitar and definitely loved recording as much as I did.

We worked on a well-received midterm, and our final was going to be a five-minute rock song, relatively commercial in form, resonating with the sonic signature of Nine Inch Nails.

I would also add a synchronized abstract visual component to it for my senior project, which Peter also commended but, again, it was never like that first song I played for him.

UCSD had an excellent student resources department, with a listing for internships by local companies. Jeff originally spotted that there was an audio internship available at a company called Four Square Productions.

He knew I had been obsessing about a Lucasfilm position and that post-production was of interest to me. He also knew I was desperate for a job and, since he would probably move back to Orange County after graduation, he suggested this was a good opportunity for me to go for.

I didn't realize it at the time, but Four Square Productions had been the top production facility in San Diego for many years. Decades, really. It was headed by John DeBello, and his silent partner was (then) Senator Steven Peace. With modest beginnings, including the low budget cult "classic" 'Attack of the Killer Tomatoes', Four Square had steadily moved up the ladder of success and had been dominating the local production scene, especially in sports and partly due to a key relationship with DirecTV.

With humble beginnings in the south of San Diego, Four Square moved north to the Kearny Mesa area and purchased a building originally designed as a health club. The squash and racquetball courts became stages. The top level had a large office for John, an ample kitchen, four editing bays, a small theater, and lots of room for salespeople and producers. The Graphics department was in an eye-popping space on the lower level. My domain, the recording studio, was in the far back corner of the top floor. It was an impressive facility, and they loved giving tours to clients.

Four Square had developed a partnership with DirecTV, and had been doing their sports show, 'DirecTV Sports This Week,' with local sports anchor Jim Lazlovic. It was a big budget affair, but not the only high dollar project that came through those doors. We did global shoots for high-end corporate clients, and brought to life future weapon systems for DARPA. This was the real deal. If I wanted an in anywhere in San Diego, it was to this company.

I was about six months away from graduating when I met Matt Melberg, Four Square's resident Sound Designer, who had posted the ad at UCSD.

On vacation with his wife in San Diego, Four Square floated a number by him that convinced him to leave his job at Todd AO in Atlanta and relocate. Todd AO is the kind of production house that cranked out broadcast television at a steady pace, and was even busier than Four Square.

Matt was intelligent, in his mid thirties, with a slight resemblance to Max Headroom. He also went to Full Sail and originally came into post-production through recording music. Born into a musical family, he said he didn't play an instrument, but after watching him for one day, I begged to differ.

I was blown away watching him work with ProTools. He played it like an instrument. With dexterity in both hands, he showed me unparalleled virtuosity with the software. I hadn't seen anyone shuttle that cursor around so quickly, manipulate files, and basically rock the house like Matt could. He was a ProTools black belt, but knew other post-production systems too. This young padawan had much to learn, and I was happy to have found a new teacher.

Life became a rhythm of trips to school, afternoons at Four Square under Matt, and BJJ at night. I began working on my senior project, which would be a three minute pop/rock song, followed by an extended coda to take it into five minute territory.

Then I would create an abstract visual component that would be synchronized to create a cool, clubby, AV experience. By this time I had already applied to Lucasfilm to take me as an intern, and I was hoping to be selected in time to work on one of the prequels in the Star Wars saga. That seemed like the career path I wanted, to be a Sound Designer for Lucasfilm or Industrial Light and Magic, and perhaps gradually work my way into film score and music.

Like many other young men my age, I anxiously anticipated Star Wars Episode 1, 2 and 3. I even stood in line at the Phantom Menace premiere in Monterey with hardcore fans surrounding me in costumes.

That movie turned out to be a mixed bag of stunning vistas, CG innovations and ten-cent dialogue. Surely the second film was going to be better.

Time would show that the issues of the first films wouldn't resolve into anything substantially better and, as Lucasfilm passed me over, another opportunity presented itself, one directly under my nose, and infinitely more practical.

Matt was a machine built for speed and, even though we had a steady stream of projects and a broadcast television show, the challenge simply wasn't there for him at Four Square. Matt and his wife wanted to start a family and move back to Atlanta (where the standard of living was considerably higher), and Todd AO played their part in luring him back with bigger bucks. Matt asked if I wanted to take over his position at Four Square, and assume the esteemed position of Sound Designer.

I leapt at the chance, rolling right into the job after graduating with honors and an A average. Having concrete FedEx deadlines and actual clients was a world away from the theory-rich environment of UCSD.

There was some serious anxiety in stepping into the top audio seat in San Diego fresh from school. Yes, I knew how to use ProTools, but I wasn't quite sure how to use the analog and digital patchbays, the DigiBeta machines, and so on.

There was a lot to learn, and a very high standard to adhere to. The eye for critical detail that the editors and producers brought to the table was mind-boggling. Totally pro, bro. I was a junior, but integral part of the team that made our projects top tier and stand out from the crowd.

I was so green coming out of school that I didn't even negotiate my salary.

The supervisor that hired me, Dan Sparks, put me at something just above the poverty line. Still, it was a paycheck, and an actual job with a legitimate future. My goal of full time employment had been obtained. Now I had to learn the job, fully, in order to keep it.

In many ways, I had arrived at adulthood. Twenty-seven years old, a college graduate, and gainfully employed. I also happened to be a purple belt in Brazilian Jiu Jitsu, a rank I had labored tirelessly for, but it was not as significant an aspect of my identity as Sound Designer at Four Square.

It was an aspect of my personal identity, a side venture which I took seriously, but ultimately a hobby and long term companion. That job was the number one priority in my life. Meeting the deadlines and professional obligations at Four Square was a responsibility I took seriously.

My real life was hosting recording sessions, making sure every production sang for our clients, and paying my dues in a professional context.

BJJ was my hobby, a fierce passion to which I was devoted, but I couldn't quite explain why. It was my secondary love, with no aspirations other than to improve and, one day, become a black belt. I wanted that skill, not just the symbol of it.

I was taking all the right steps to get there, and my professional stability ensured my ability to train. I continued to chip away at the work ahead of me.

CHAPTER 7

A PATH
BEYOND THOUGHT

A PATH BEYOND THOUGHT

I walked into the kitchen of the Gala house and saw a bright yellow flyer on the table. It had just come in the mail.

The HCK All Comers Tourney.

I felt my heart skip a beat, and something in me brightened.

I wanted to compete!

The tournament would be my first competition as a purple belt, and everything about it felt right. People had been telling me I was at that next level for a while, but I had just recently been promoted. My expectations were low, and my motivation quite high. Everything was in place for me to train seriously.

I lifted. I sprinted. I sparred intensely and often. The training should have been misery, but, strangely enough, it didn't feel that way. The physical coursework was a challenge I was ready to take on. At this point, I had enough experience to know how to train and not wreck myself in the process. Perhaps most importantly, I had learned how to calm my mind.

My mind had been wild and completely untamed for so many of my previous competitions. Nervousness. Insomnia. Expectations of what I wanted to do and worries about what my opponent might do. Mix it all together and it's a cocktail for subpar performance. Lots of energy was wasted just feeding my anxiety. My mind itself was a hole in my game.

Then, in the middle of training, I had an epiphany.

The more I cut my mind out of it, the better I would do.

I just had to trust myself. Not trust my mind, but trust my body. My body already knew what to do, where to go, how to move. That's what the training was for.

My body would react correctly once it hit the mat. I just had to believe that it would. I spent thousands of hours on the mat, in all kinds of positions, with a myriad of body types, and I had earned the confidence that only comes from submitting skilled opponents repeatedly.

Don't think, just do. Or something very close to that.

I had plenty of time to prepare for the competition, and there was a bonus: as an HCK sponsored athlete, Dan Camarillo would be there, not only to compete, but also to do an exhibition match with his brother Dave, a fierce brown belt under the legendary Ralph Gracie.

Dan and I shot a few e-mails back and forth leading up to the tournament. He had been leading a group of students in Bakersfield and, if possible, he would be entering the brown belt division. So cool! He would do well in any division he entered. Dan was the man.

A group of people from the Harris Academy were heading up to the tournament that Saturday morning, but I went up a day early, crashing with a mentor of mine, John Tessier.

A lifelong martial artist, John has studied under some of the best in the business. I chilled at his house, then got lost in Los Angeles trying to meet up with Dan and his girlfriend for a drink. We eventually connected, but I headed home early and was just looking forward to the tournament.

The event was well organized, with a slew of white and blue belt competitors. For an inaugural tourney, the turnout was impressive, but it there were only a few purple belts to compete that day: Dan Camarillo from Ralph Gracie, David Horlick from James Boran, and myself from Roy Harris. I was informed that we would be put into a single, combined weight class, in a round robin format.

What? I have to fight Dan Camarillo? The Armhunter was extremely dangerous.

The prospect of facing my idol in competition should have left me frozen in place. But on that day I simply accepted it. This was happening. There was nothing I could do. I couldn't back out. Panicking now would not help in any way.

One of my teammates, Michio Grubbs, asked how I felt about facing Dan, probably expecting an emotional breakdown.

I simply replied, "Well, I can always go for the foot."

Mr. Harris is renown for his leg lock expertise, winning fourteen of his twenty-one competitions with the straight foot lock alone, and this lineage was an advantage I possessed.

Perhaps the only one. But it's nice to have one.

I was team leader that day, coaching teammates in the white and blue belt divisions, and even leaving the tournament to get additional ice for the injured. I wasn't really thinking about myself, or that match, so I just strolled through the day, easy as a man can be before his execution. The match was happening, so there was no use in getting worked up about it.

Since there were so few of us, the purple belt matches were treated like a super fight, with all eyes on the mat.

Dan and David Horlick are up first. In under two minutes, Dan finishes David with a helicopter arm lock from guard. The essence of the technique is this:

Dan, while on his back, scooped David up with his legs and almost lifted him over his head, which prompted David to extend his arms to catch his balance. Once the arm was exposed, Dan rotated David ninety degrees with his feet, shot his hips into position and finished with an elbow lock. He used manipulation of balance (kuzushi) to create an opportunity to finish the fight. Beautiful, deadly jujutsu.

Dan had a short recovery period and we were up next. Even though his match was just a few minutes long, Dan used some energy getting his opponent into the air.

Now it was my time to step on the mat.

Let's do this.

I could not have been more prepared.

The match began. I grabbed his lapel with my left hand and pulled half guard. This was critical. I knew that he could throw me, rather easily, and it would be during that moment of impact that he'd sit back for the submission, and The Armhunter would take another prize.

But not today. Better to pull guard and play the game a little longer.

I loosened my legs and Dan cut his right knee through, passing my guard as I spun to my knees. He stepped over my upper body while his other leg hooked my shoulder, then he fell to the ground. This is a classic set up for the rolling arm lock in Judo.

He was waiting to finish and the match had only just begun!

My right hand grabbed my left bicep, protecting my arm from being locked out, allowing me to get my knees underneath me, where I had more leverage and movement options. Dan gave up on the arm lock and sat to guard, which was a strong position for him. He shin swept me, but I managed to catch my balance at the last possible second.

That sweep created enough space for him to free his knee and attack my back. Sensing this, I sat to guard and immediately attacked with a sleeve choke.

My left hand pushed his head down and sank my wrist into his neck, gripping tightly on his lapel, locking my own wrist under my elbow and trying to finish the choke.

But I didn't have his hips immobilized, so Dan simply lifted them up and punched my elbow off of his head, breaking the submission.

I re-attack with a triangle. Dan dropped his hips and hid his head, giving nothing for my legs to ensnarl, controlling the cuff of my pant leg, nullifying my attack. His defenses were impregnable.

Dan back stepped to pass my guard to the left, with his right hand on my gi between the shoulder blades. He pulled his leg free, squared himself and then pushed his knee across my hips to secure the pass.

This is the moment where total commitment counted. Had I not been fighting someone I respected so much, it's possible I would have conceded that guard pass and simply regrouped from side control. But because of my admiration for him, because I knew how skilled he was, I had to fight continuously.

Every second. Every millimeter. I could not quit.

As Dan slid his shin to knee on belly position, I brought both of my knees to my chest, and angled in to face him.

One knee came under his thigh, the other went over. His leg was now trapped between my knees. I circled my legs into my torso and shifted his weight backwards. Dan's ankle rolled underneath him, and he had no choice but to jump away to catch his balance. As I felt him retreat I followed him up to my knees to fill the void and possibly take his back.

Protecting against this, Dan pulled guard, and referee Fernando Vasconcuelos awarded me two points for the reversal. I was up in the match against my BJJ idol.

Dan had a very aggressive guard. Inverting himself, he looked for triangles and re-spun to standard guard position at will. I couldn't take any chances. Holding on to his knee with an unshakeable grip, I overlapped pressures and controlled his leg by placing my shin over his inner thigh. Pinning his leg with my bodyweight, I sat back for a straight foot lock.

He elevated his hip to free himself, but couldn't get above my knees, which were clamped tightly on his leg. He peeled my ankle off of his hip with his hand, then slid over my shin and on to the mat, executing a textbook escape.

As he moved his hips to the right to free himself, I began setting up a guard pass. I leapt past his guard to north south, but didn't really have control and Dan immediately spun to replace guard.

Fernando Vasconcuelos then pulled us from our exact positions to restart in the center of the mat.

Sprawled out as low as I could get, I began to drive forward, even though his shins were on my shoulders. As his hips were driven higher, he rolled on to his shoulders and I jumped past his legs.

He swung up to replace guard and I blocked his knee with my head, pulling hard on his lapel to keep the space between us closed. With my head driving down, I grabbed his heel and sat back to a straight knee bar.

He rolled with the momentum, changed the angle, and negated my leg lock attempt yet again.

I was trying my best to pass his guard, but it was extremely difficult. Dan knew time was running out and, knowing that he was down on points, he became more aggressive.

Which is scary.

He pulled hard towards his head and elevated me with his hands and feet, hoping I'd offer an exposure for the helicopter arm lock. But rather than resisting, I did a rather unseemly cartwheel out onto my hands and then back to my feet. Thank you gymnastics.

We started from standing with less than thirty seconds on the clock, but being on our feet was one of the worst positions possible against a Judo champion, especially this one.

I gripped his lapel with my left hand. He counter gripped on my left arm and collar.

The moment he released his grip from my elbow, I grabbed his right arm and jumped into the air.

There was no thought in this. Only action. Direct action.

My calf chopped down on his neck, breaking his posture. By the time we hit the ground, my legs were already crossed and squeezing. Once my knee locked behind my foot, the triangle choke was set.

Dan took a big step over my body while trying to counter, but my leg positioning was secure. I continued to apply pressure with my legs. I knew he wouldn't escape. It was my number one submission, on my best side. The odds were in my favor.

I could tell Dan didn't want to tap. In that moment, there was no joy in the victory. No elation. Just one thought came through,

"It's OK. It's OK to tap."

To have your hero lose by your own hand was somehow heartbreaking.

Dan tapped and I released the choke. We both rolled onto our backs to catch our breath. I stood up and extended a hand to help my friend.

He accepted and we stood together on the mat. The referee lifted my arm to the crowd for the victory. There was applause. People couldn't believe how much of an upset this was.

I could scarcely believe it myself.

A few minutes later, I knelt next to Dan and his family, asking him to cheer for me in the next match. He looked at me and roared, "Just go out there and beat him!"

Energized beyond belief, I strode onto the mat for the match and shook David's Horlick's hand. My mind was clear and, without conscious thought, I attacked with a flying arm lock. As my hips hit the ground, I slid past his legs to the finishing position. I leaned back and he tapped.

I had unknowingly attacked his injured arm, and apologized for doing so after the match. I don't believe in kicking a man while he's down, but apparently I believe in tapping someone when they're injured. At least subconsciously.

So there it was. A peak experience. A transcendent moment. Action with no thought. The smallest satori.

As if that wasn't enough, I also received two awards for my performance: one for the fastest submission (15 seconds) and another for the most technical fighter. As prizes, I received two HCK gi's, a white one for myself and a blue one which I gave to Brad.

Afterwards, having lunch alone in a random Korean restaurant, I phoned Brad and left a voicemail telling him I had won my match by flying triangle against Daniel Camarillo. He later shared that he thought the message was a joke, and that I was simply too embarrassed to tell him the actual result.

I drove home, naturally wired, wondering what had just happened to me.

I emerged from that competition with two insights.

First, the victory made me believe in myself. I knew that I was capable, not only of losing and winning, but also of great performances. I knew how good Dan was. He brought out my best and, having been raised to that level, even if only once, I was changed. Earlier in my journey, it would have been impossible. Dan only tapped once before in his career (to Tyrone Glover, by choke). This win was proof that I was actually good at this jiu jitsu thing. Finally.

The second epiphany was more profound: that, in the act of tapping, you could empower another person to believe in themselves. We are all capable of great things. The harder-earned the victory, the more certain that belief becomes.

Analyzing the situation, other circumstances also contributed to this victory:

I believed in my game. I had trained hard and my conditioning level was high. I had rested the night before in a comfortable environment. I had also seen hours of footage of Dan competing on tape, in Judo and BJJ, which had been a gift from Kim. I knew his game, but he wasn't that familiar with mine. Plus, I had made a huge leap in ability since the last time we had seen each other.

Dan Camarillo is one of the most talented martial artists I have met. He's an enormous inspiration, and even deadlier as a black belt than he was at purple.

I thank him again for sharing the mat with me that day and allowing me to discover part of who I am.

I am deeply grateful.

CHAPTER 8
THE PRICE OF SECOND PLACE

悪戦苦闘

THE PRICE OF SECOND PLACE

My next tournament experience was the opposite of the HCK event.

The Westside Submission Tournament was hosted by Chris Brennan, a black belt under John De La O, who would hold round robin tournaments at his academy in Orange County.

Not only was the skill level of competitors high in Southern California, this tournament attracted a particularly wide range of competitors because it had no uniforms, no belt levels, and only weight categories.

I felt like I had properly prepared for the tournament, and also knew that it was possible I would face one of my teammates and friends, Michio Grubbs, in the pool of competitors. Michio was a purple belt under Mr. Harris and had his own school north of San Diego. I loved training with him and his team, and he would prove an invaluable ally on this quest.

I remember driving to the tournament on a beautiful Saturday morning, just beaming inside.

"Competition day," I thought to myself, "is the a celebration of the sacrifice and dedication you just invested."

It was a serene journey up there. I checked in at Next Generation. I attended the rules meeting. My Russian brother, Serge, was living in LA and came down to support me with his friend Alex.

I was excited about having a great performance, especially with the momentum of the HCK tournament.

Here's how it went down:

First Match: I'm the opener in our nine-man division. My opponent and I shook hands and he immediately shot for a double leg takedown. I went to full guard, and started to angle off for arm locks and triangles. I threw up my left leg over his shoulder, shooting for a triangle, and he buried his elbow in my crotch.

Like good parenting, it was firm and remorseless. It blocked my hips from coming up any higher, and the authority with which he drove the elbow in made me realize he would not be moving it out of the way. My crotch, my problem.

I wasn't wearing a cup, so to alleviate the pressure I rolled backwards to replace guard. This is exactly what he wanted, as he quickly took my back, with hooks, and slid his arm around my neck for a rear naked choke.

Boom. This guy finished me like a boss. I had been defeated, rather easily.

Bottom line is that I wasn't ready. I was still too cold. Still too kind. Still climbing the arousal curve. My friend was at his peak. It was a bloodbath, and I brought white sheets.

Physiologically, I wasn't ready to make contact with somebody who was that focused, sharp, and ready to go. We had different levels of intensity and I was overwhelmed. I needed to get in the game. Now.

Second Match: I wasn't going to lose this one. With a talented purple belt named Rick Estrada. This entire match was a battle. He was working a variation of the guillotine choke, which attacked my windpipe rather than my arteries. I almost tapped several times as I felt my throat ripping apart, but hung in there.

There was a scramble as he attempted to take my back and I rolled out, emerging on top. I passed his guard to side control, then went to knee on belly. While attempting to switch sides of my knee on belly position, I made a critical error and gave too much space. Rick felt this and wrapped my leg for a heel hook. I escaped the first attempt and he switched to the other leg, with a hearty stomp to my crotch. I was sensing a theme. I tapped quickly as he expertly applied the heel hook. It was very tight.

"This is not good..." I thought to myself. "This is not what I imagined. Two matches in and six to go. This could be a long day."

Hey, didn't I just win my last tournament against an amazing competitor? What just happened here? Defeated twice, with friends and supporters watching. This was no good. Something had to change.

So I changed my mind. My expectations. I simply said to myself, "Well, it's all just experience now" and let go of my expectation of winning the gold. I let go of my ego which had come through those doors, strong and intact, before being ball stomped, heel hooked, and choked into submission.

There was no attachment going forward. It was just experience. I wasn't even going to try to be perfect since it didn't matter. Nothing counted anymore.

Third Match: the guy dropped back to open guard. I skipped past his legs and took his back. I was not that nice. I pressed to be aggressive and inflicted my will on him. I made that choke happen. Victory. At least I got a win. My blood was finally pumping.

Fourth Match: against one of Dean Lister's students. He pulled guard and I passed it easily. He rolled to his knees, and I spun to the back. I try to finish by rear naked choke, then an arm lock, but lost it. He dove for a toe-hold but I went with it, didn't tap and gave him a nice cross face in return. I remained on the hunt and eventually caught him in a triangle choke, then an arm lock with only seconds to spare. Two wins.

Fifth Match: with one of the two "Gentleman Grapplers" in my division. I spoke with their coach earlier and discovered he trained out of his garage. I was pretty sure he was the father of one of the young men. I went straight to my "A" game at this point and put the guy in a triangle. He was so thin and lanky there wasn't enough mass to get a proper choke. No meat, all bone, was making my life difficult. He was trapped in the submission for several minutes, and I eventually switched to an arm lock for the W. Three wins.

Sixth Match: Match of day. As soon as I stood up to get out on the mat, Michio pumped me up. "THIS is it. This is THE match right here." I knew it would be tough, but I still didn't expect what the Berzerker brought to the table. Nicknamed by his fight shorts with "BERZEK" printed on the back, this guy was a highly skilled, highly explosive wrestler. He was going crazy on the competition as well, and he hadn't lost yet.

Our referee, Jeremy Williams, signals us to begin. I'm taken down in a split second by a lightening double leg. He did a well-rehearsed feint, a level change, and a beautiful shot with full commitment. That was a black belt level shot. It was a shot so good, I didn't have any delusions of being able to stop it going forward. He owned me there.

After he took me down and began driving into me, one thing became perfectly clear: he was the strongest person I had ever wrestled in my life. By far. I knew I would never beat him with power. I was the willow branch and he was the snow. My only choice was to yield and find another way to win.

His strategy was typical for wrestlers: get the takedown, nullify the guard and stand back up. Repeat as necessary. In a tournament like this, where it's two points for a submission win, a point each for a draw, and nothing for a loss, our friend was likely just going for the draw. And maybe some target practice with his double leg.

He smothered my guard, always moving but never really trying to pass. I almost swept him to reverse the position, and he took that opportunity to stand back up. I stood up as well, and he returned the favor with another double leg, plus a big slam. A big fucking slam. That's the bonus. I see how this is going.

THIS IS THE match. It was power vs. technique. Good vs. evil. He could not have been more aggressive; mad dogging me with his eyes and mocking me before taking his shot. Not a normal level of animosity, even considering the combative circumstances.

Jiu jitsu is about adaptation, and I had to figure a way out to win, because I was losing badly. I would never overpower him, even if I were fresh. I burned a lot of gas in the earlier matches, and this recent beating wasn't helping things either. But the thought of quitting never occurred to me. I kept fighting. I had to find a way. I knew I could.

I could hear Michio sternly urging me to "Take charge Roy, take charge." I moved forward with a foot sweep and got an over-hook on his arm. I threatened the Bezerker with an uchimata, and he caught his balance with his legs split, with a wide base. As he stabilized, I pushed his left wrist back, jumped into the air and crossed my legs over his neck.

The flying triangle was set and we came crashing back to earth. Everything I needed to finish was there. Legs were locked. I just needed to move his arm from the left side to the right side of my body. I raise my hips and slid his arm over, but it only made it halfway.

His elbow was driving into the pit of my stomach. It hurt like a motherfucker. He was pushing that elbow in as deep into my stomach as he could to block me from completing the choke.

Sometimes an opponent will recognize that they're so deeply embedded into a submission that they give up. This is a smart training strategy, since there's no need to waste energy or risk an injury. Resetting the pieces once checkmate has been achieved in an intelligent approach. The goal is to play, not delay your inevitable demise.

But this wasn't training, and our friend was defiant. He wasn't giving up. He'd rather go to sleep than tap out. You run into this from time to time.

Thirty seconds left. This had to end soon. Even with his elbow driving into my center, I squeezed my legs and pulled on his head as hard as I could. It was killing me to tighten the triangle with his elbow in my gut. But my calculus was that the pain would be temporary, and the victory forever. Alas, our poor friend still would not tap.

As I pulled on his head, he reached out and grabbed my wrist. A touch of panic had set in, he didn't realize the exposure he had just given me. I pulled my hand away from his head, and he kept holding on to the wrist.

Him grabbing me is another way of me grabbing him. I took his fist he grabbed me with, hooked it with my elbow, and threw my leg over his face for the arm bar.

The arm lock was set. I bridged up and over my right shoulder, squeezed my knees, and pushed my hip against his elbow. Off balance, even this savvy and strong competitor couldn't fight the leverage, leaving him no choice but to tap out.

The room went wild. It was a sick move against an unbelievably tough competitor. Everyone there appreciated what just happened.

As I stood up, I felt a mix of triumph and intense relief. My opponent gave me a thumbs up and congratulated me on the victory. I solved the riddle and showed serious heart in that match.

Seventh Match: against the second of the "Gentleman Grapplers." I pulled guard, put him in a triangle and finished with an arm lock.

Done. I'm over it. Get me home, please.

My teammate, Jeff Yurk, met me at a restaurant halfway home to San Diego. As I sat down to feed the machine, I realized I was having difficulty swallowing. Serious difficulty. My throat was ripped and starting to swell, and I knew it was from that ten-finger guillotine variation in the second match.

Eating was terrible. Scratchy and rough, scraping past a bottleneck in the middle of my throat. I sat there in the booth and had to ask myself some difficult questions, like:

What the fuck was I doing? Sacrificing my body for a two-dollar medal? I actually paid and drove a long distance for the opportunity to get beaten up.

Even Michio, an ex professional body builder with tremendous conditioning, dropped out of that tournament from an injury. It didn't make any sense to me. I won five out of 7 seven matches by submission, but at what price? I knew I was good. What lengths did I have to go to prove it? At what point does the application of the art on the competition scene begin to diminish your quality of life? This is a critical calculus for all practitioners of combat sports to engage in honestly.

A few weeks later, in a private lesson with Mr. Harris, I shared this thought:

"Mr. Harris, I don't think I want to compete anymore. I'm actually paying money to take the risk of being injured. It just doesn't make any sense to me."

Much to my surprise, he calmly stated "Good. I've been waiting for you to say that."

So many other instructors would have tried to talk me out of that stance. Now that I was developing a bit of a reputation on the SoCal scene, some teachers would have pushed me to fly the flag, represent the school, and bring honor and glory to my academy.

But his perspective was just the opposite. What's the point? Who was the champion from last year? Who got silver? Very few people know and, if you don't care about it, then you shouldn't be doing it. It's a hobby, people. Life is short. Use your energy wisely.

I was still at Four Square, still applying myself and getting exponentially more competent in the studio. Being a sound designer was my real job, my actual vocation, that earned real dollars, provided creative satisfaction and professional respect. I enjoyed teaching the little bit that I did at the Harris Academy, but I was starting to lose some of the drive that kept me in jiu jitsu for so long. I was spending more time with my girlfriend and enjoying a little bit of this salary, which I'd never had before. I could have easily drifted away.

Then something happened. Brad and I both received an email from Mr.

Harris, telling us that if we applied ourselves, and kept our minds on a few key steps, that we could both be brown belts the next year. Brown belts!

He encouraged us to print out the email, post it where we would see it everyday, and chip away at the advice he had laid out so clearly. We each needed a submission that we owned, we needed to work on our top game and guard passing, and we had to be able to close the distance if our opponent decided to retreat. He outlined other steps as well, but that was the gist. Brad and I both taped the email to our computer screens and studied it everyday.

A brown belt is just a heavily seasoned purple belt who's one step ahead. Blue to purple is a radical transformation of creating a complete game. Purple to brown is the same game, filled out and expanded in some areas, but delivered with more authority. More efficiently.

Finding those nooks, crannies and body positions which increase efficiency, takes time. Movements can be combined to shave steps off the checklist of critical components for a technique, and these must be practiced. It takes a lot of rolling and a lot of mat time to be able to discover things on your own, improvise attacks, see new openings and options, but you'll get there if you keep at it.

It took years of hard work and dedication, but Brad and both I earned our brown belts from Mr. Harris in multi-hour, grueling physical exams.

Every other aspect of our lives remained the same, but Brad and I understood the gravitas of what we had accomplished, together.

CHAPTER 9

WRESTLING CAMP

KU WA RAKU NO TANE

苦は楽の種

NO PAIN, NO GAIN

WRESTLING CAMP

Brown belt is arguably the best place to be in jiu jitsu.

This is the time where you really tighten the basics, with the aim of perfect execution.

It's a study in solid, well-grounded movements that generate pressure from both top and bottom positions.

You can still be tapped at brown belt, but it's pretty rare. If you put yourself in bad positions purposely and make yourself vulnerable, it happens. Which you should be doing anyway. A fresh brown belt can tap anybody who walks on the mat. Regardless of their background. This is an extremely empowering, and slightly addictive feeling.

Brown belt is also a time of confidence. People have been gunning for you for so long that you've learned to deal with a myriad of attacks efficiently. You start to block people before they even get going. Different challengers require different responses and you need to start deducing their skill sets by their body type and the way that they move. Brown belt is tactical problem solving, and far less often about "how to do" a specific technique. But there's still lessons to be had. You're not done yet.

It's also a time of observation. By this point you know the steps in your game plan, the routines and subroutines in your jiu jitsu code so well that you're often waiting for your opponent to catch up.

Many challenges have come your way over the years and you now realize that you can handle them. You adapt to each situation. It's not effortless, but it happens. Most of the time, you're on top. There will always be guys bigger than you are. You can't match their strength, so don't even try. Just use your body more efficiently than they do, make them carry your weight, tire them out and finish the fight.

Simple. Direct. You're not just doing it, you're doing it efficiently. Better to be patient than overly aggressive when it's a serious duel. You play the percentages, and sometimes that means being conservative. The game has finally become just as strategic as it is physical.

Brown belt is where balance is achieved. Physically, technically, and tactically.

Countering the final defenses of a submission is one area that should capture the attention of a brown belt. It can take years before you can truly study small subjects like that in depth in jiu jitsu.

Take the defenses to the rear naked choke, as an example.

This requires you to reliably open and pass your opponent's guard, then turn them, or create an exposure of their back, and secure yourself with your legs. Then you can focus on getting the choke on from their back.

There's a pyramid of skills that support you. As they defend, you mentally catalogue their reactions and attempt or devise counters to their counters. The work takes place at the very last stages of the equation.

Your awareness level at brown belt is quite high. You can play the game politely, and appreciate how others play it too. A brown belt may be able to catch their instructor occasionally. Don't let it go to your head. This is how it should be.

At this point, a brown belt understands the process of skill acquisition, so the real challenge is finding which techniques, movements, and tactics should be experimented with, embraced, then programmed in.

Cross training becomes much more appealing. In fact, it's necessary. So you become the perfect student. Already lethal, so there's nothing to prove. You have an awareness of where the holes in your game are, and you now know how to train and cover those gaps.

This is a perfect time to reach out to experts in those areas where you're lacking and make a pilgrimage to train with them. You're not trying to prove anything to anyone else. It's solely for your own education.

All of this must be done with great respect and discretion to your original teacher. Of course. Always.

Wrestling Camp

Wrestling camp was my pilgrimage. My wrestling needed work. My Judo was OK, but wrestling was more applicable in no gi situations, and I needed a better understanding of attacks and defenses, seen through the lens of real wrestling practices.

By immersing myself in the art, I hoped to understand the wrestler's mentality, techniques, and training methods.

I researched a ton of different wrestling camps, and one of them seemed perfect. It was just north of San Diego, in a small town of Ocean Side, at The Academy by the Sea campus. The Academy was a prep school for boys during the school year, and opened itself up to various recreational and educational camps during the summer. Located on the beach itself, it was definitely a convenient and beautiful choice.

The staff was well qualified. It was going to be run by Mark Munoz, a 2001 NCAA wrestling champion at 197 pounds, and now, years later, a formidable middleweight in the UFC (and a source of pride and inspiration for the Philippines).

I gave Mark a call and left a message with his wife. Mark called back that afternoon and I explained my situation: I was a jiu jitsu brown belt looking to improve my wrestling, and this seemed a great way to do it.

He understood completely and welcomed me into attending the five day session, as a bona fide camper.

I arrived on a perfect SoCal day. Blue skies and sun over manicured, green lawns at the Academy by the Sea. I registered at a fold out table in front of the gym, and met Mark and his wife. I was assigned to the counselor's quarters, and I'd be bunking with all of the UC Davis wrestling team.

Believe me, I stuck out. At six feet, two inches tall, I'm definitely bigger than the junior high kids. A twenty-nine year old camper is not the norm at these events.

All the campers were brought out onto a huge field, where the counselors were introduced. Then they broke us into teams, and we did wind sprint relays up and down the field, sometimes carrying people on our backs, before sending us into the gym.

We drilled, shooting and sprawling on the mats, and it was clear to me at that point on the first day that these camps were into tiring us out. Even though we were doing techniques and receiving instruction, it was not what I would call a technique oriented training session like a jiu jitsu class. Gross motor movements and a lot of calorie expenditure were the objectives.

I also found out that sleeping there wasn't going to work. I was staying with the other adults, yes, but the Davis wrestling team was hyperactive at night. College jocks run amok, away from home, ready to fucking party. I didn't get a lot of sleep that first night.

By the end of the second day, I was toasted. My muscles were breaking down badly, and I need some protein drinks, stat. The food at camp was pretty good, but still inadequate for the rate of catabolism I found myself in.

At the earliest opportunity, I drove to Trader Joe's, stocked up on protein drinks and bananas, and went home to sleep in my own damn bed. I sat on the edge of the bed and seriously contemplated that this may have been a mistake.

Wrestling camp was way more intense, physically grueling, and even socially disorienting than I had ever anticipated.

I wasn't really the audio engineer who hosted clients and recorded talent, or the brown belt instructor with his own grappling class.

I was a novice wrestler, around a bunch of junior high and high school kids, pairing up with a teenager everyone called Doyle for his resemblance to the character in Adam Sandler's classic comedy "Billy Madison." Doyle's approach to wrestling was more of the beat them down and intimidate them horribly in the first round mentality. He went really hard out of the gate of our sparring sessions and got launched with an uchimata for his efforts.

Mark was the head coach for UC Davis, and Uriah Faber was his assistant. Urijiah was still young in his Mixed Martial Arts career, with a record of eight and zero at that time .

I first heard of Urijiah's name after he defeated a brown belt named Rami Boukai in King of the Cage, a local MMA promotion that held fights in the lush expanse of Hemet California.

Rami was a student of Chris Brennan, and I met him when he dropped into the UCSD BJJ class. Rami had good jiu jitsu, so I knew that Urijiah was a force to be reckoned with, even though I'd never seen him in action.

After a few days of running on the beach at 6 a.m. and getting in the groove with the wrestling mentality and practice structure, I was enjoying it. The counselors understood my motivations for training, and I'd hit them with questions.

Uriah had received his purple belt under Cassio Werneck, and was rolling during camp with some guys, but I stayed away. The wrestling was hard enough for me, that's what I was there for, and this exposure to wrestling was enlightening. There were techniques that I didn't need to add to my jiu jitsu game, like leg rides and turnovers, but seeing an alternate approach in order to accomplish a specific goal (pinning under tight time constraints rather than a submission victory with no time limits) was eye opening.

My best technical takeaway was this: the wrestling approach to the inside trip trapped your opponent's ankle behind your knee, while the Judo variation involved sweeping their leg out from underneath them with a J motion. Both are good, but I found the wrestling approach to be effective for me. Higher percentage. Trap that ankle, put your hip on their knee, push out and take them down.

There were modest technical gains made on my part, but the wrestling mentality made a larger impression. The guest instructors for the camp, many of them national champions and friends of Mark, talked about their own struggles.

One recalled how his mother's cancer diagnosis spurred him to "stop being such a pussy," and gave him the kick in the pants he needed for victory at the highest level of collegiate athletics, spurring him on to a national championship.

Mark recalled one of his personal struggles, suffering a harrowing foot injury as a child. Mark was in a full sprint, playing capture the flag as a kid at summer camp, when he stepped into a hole and shattered his ankle.

He was taken to the hospital but, for whatever reason, there was an issue with his medical insurance, so he was shuttled to another hospital, who also turned him away.

This went on to the point where Mark was on the verge of losing his foot. Finally, through no small miracle, one doctor took him in and worked out the details later.

Little did that doctor know that he would be to thank for a national wrestling championship and the many mixed martial arts victories Mr. Munoz went on to win. Kindness can be powerful, and ever unfolding. Consider this.

Wrestling camp can be summarized in four inspirational quotes: "Quitters never win, and winners never quit." "Embrace the grind." "Outwork your opponent." "Stop being such a pussy."

There were many variations of this theme, and it was a powerful reminder to me, as a grown man, that you never stop paying your dues.

There are level changes in wrestling, education, and professional life. Hard work will always be necessary to achieve your goals. No shortcuts.

Tyrone Glover rolled into the camp, on several occasions, with a couple of brothers from the Gracie Academy. Tyrone and Uriah wrestled together in high school, and Tyrone was the first person to suggest that Uriah get into MMA. Now Uriah was returning the favor by setting up sparring partners in preparation for his match against Din Thomas in Japan, using the UC Davis wrestling team. I was trying to nap one afternoon on my assigned bunk, and Uriah burst into the dorm, rallying the guys on the team- "C'mon let's do this! Let's go!"

Even though I was annoyed by the volume of his entrance, I was also really impressed at the passion Uriah had for his friend. He really wanted to make it a good training for Tyrone. It was tough training with stud athletes and serious intensity. He actually cared, and you could tell. Respect.

I was there the night that Tyrone got his black belt, just a few months earlier. He moved from Santa Barbara to San Diego, and took a job as the BJJ instructor at City Boxing.

He had posted at the "In The Guard" forum that all schools were welcome that night, no drop in fee necessary. They were having a visit from his instructor, Ricardo Franjinha Miller, and coming down with him was a promising young purple belt named Jeff Glover, who had been killing everyone in the tournaments. Before he was known as "The Pipelayer," Glover was most definitely "The Giant Killer."

I rolled down there with my friends Jeff Baldwin and Alicia Anthony from the Harris Academy. The mats were full, and the vibe was especially good.

Tyrone, an African American specimen with jackpot genetics, had one of the most stunning girlfriends I'd ever seen. With alabaster skin, she set up a compelling contrast, and she couldn't take her eyes off of Tyrone for a second.

I had never seen a female so captivated by a male. Even in those nature shows. The dude was a pimp.

At the end of the class at City Boxing, Franjinha called Tyrone up to the front of the group and revealed his surprise: a black belt.

Franjinha shared his story of coming to this country with no money, a pregnant wife, and a dream. Now here he was, with his son running around on the mats, awarding his first black belt to an incredibly talented and dedicated student.

I was actually seeing a dream coming true. Both teacher and student briefly shed tears (which they tried to restrain) as the belt was tied around Tyrone's waist. They hugged, then Franjinha threw him to the ground with a hip toss. That was the tradition. That was a transmission that I was able to witness. It was an honor to be there.

But that's not where it ended. A very dark brown belt was awarded to Jeff Glover. Then Tyrone, Jeff, and myself got on our backs to form 3 groups, and played King of the Mountain, where students work to pass our guards, and we looked to sweep or submit them. Then we all rolled. It was a beautiful night.

Dreams came true, for teacher, student, and another young jedi, Jeff Glover, who would go on to become arguably Franjinha's best known student, no gi world champion, as well as a creative instructor and competitor.

But back to camp. It was hard training but, in talking to the kids, it was clear that they loved this camp. Some called it the best they had ever been to, partially because it was actually less physically grueling than other wrestling camps, like the J. Robinson retreat.

By day three I had locked into the groove, spending the night in my own bed back in San Diego, and driving up the next morning to be there for practice. But Southern California traffic is a fickle beast and, one morning, I was snarled in the commute, tiptoeing into the gymnasium about ten minutes late. Roll call had already taken place, and everyone there knew I was late.

Mark had to make an example of me. I completely understood and supported his decision to publicly discipline me, along with the other camper who was caught outside after lights out.

The kid and I did a seriously whacked workout, in front of the entire gymnasium, that made Claudio's look like a cake walk. Perhaps the worst exercise was the one Mark called "lame dogs", facedown, walking on two hands and one foot, and doing laps around the gym, with the other leg extended behind you in the air.

That's a serious wake up call to your low back. I was dripping with sweat by the end of it, and one of the counselors grudgingly said "good job." It was punitive, it was effective, and I was not late again, even though there was only one day left at camp, I made sure I was there early.

We were set to have a small wresting tournament on the last day. The night before the tournament, I stayed with a beautiful girl I was dating who lived in Carlsbad, just a short distance away.

It's a classic war ritual: you are going to battle the next morning, so you share one last night with a fair maiden, and enter the fight with a clear yet relaxed awareness. That clarity is exactly what gives you the edge. It's the tantric path to mushin (no mind).

I arrived early the next morning, and was still quite sore from the punitive workout I'd endured. But the fact that my body ached helped quell any anxiety I was holding on to. No matter how tough my matches might be, it would still be easier than what I had endured yesterday. My opponent would never make me suffer as much as those jump squats or lame dogs, that much I was sure of.

All campers lined up, heaviest to lightest, and the people standing next to you formed the group of three that you'd be wrestling. I had a couple of high

BECOMING THE BLACK BELT

school kids to contend with, and pinned the first one for the W. The second kid was really squirrely, and even though I was close to pinning him, I ended up winning on points.

Some of the kids that watched the matches called me Spiderman for the way I used all my limbs. Uriah also approached me afterwards and told me that learning wrestling this way was a very intelligent approach. He was quite cool and I appreciated all the guidance he had offered me that week.

I drove down to Coronado Island after the camp was over. It's difficult to describe the exuberance that I felt, but it was something almost childlike, as if anything were possible.

There was a euphoria from having taken on a challenge so difficult, so utterly unnecessary, and so vastly removed from the rhythms of the working world. The twenty-nine year old camper had done it, though I don't recommend it to the faint of heart.

CHAPTER 10

MEETING THE GURU

運命を制す

MEETING THE GURU

Four Square had me working fifty weeks a year, with only 2 for vacation, so I did my best to maximize my time off.

The first half of this vacation was putting in work at the wrestling camp. The last couple of days would be spent visiting my friend Dave in Northern California.

The plan was to hit a hot springs and take in some well-deserved relaxation before returning to the real world.

I knew Dave from my Seibukan Jujutsu days. During my time as an uchideshi, he would occasionally drop in for training, living in the dojo for a week or two.

Dave was primarily a web development guy, occasionally moonlighting as a magician, but what was really unique about Dave was that he had a guru. He casually mentioned it years ago in a car ride to Mendocino to attend a seminar.

The idea of having a guru seemed pretty strange to me. Bowing before a teacher was something that we did in martial arts all the time, but I seemed to have an easier time with that habit, in that context.

But having Dave refer to this guy as his lord and spiritual master struck me as over the top. Apparently, he was some kind of god-man, the culmination of the worlds religions and the prophecies in one single, beloved being.

Even if it's not true, that's a cool thing to put on your resume.

Dave gave me a call and invited me to see his spiritual teacher. His guru had just returned to his Northern California retreat center. He had been living on his personal island in Fiji, which was received as a gift from one of his wealthy devotees.

He would be seeing members of the public for the first time in many years.

Dave assured me that this was a big deal. He even half-jokingly suggested that I steal the money if I have to. That's how precious this spiritual opportunity was. That's how divine.

I was definitely heading up for the hot springs, but I did hold it in the back of my mind that I could probably fit in an orientation. If I didn't like the presentation and wanted to opt out early, Dave and I would just soak.

I have a thing for hot springs. Taking the waters from mother earth is a timeless, and clinically beneficial way to recuperate. I see it as a penetrating heat massage. After fifty weeks of work, plus wrestling camp, it was definitely needed and highly anticipated.

I flew to Sacramento, Dave picked me up, and we headed back to his place. He had a couple of roommates, both devotees. Nice people, but the guy looked pretty pale. Ghostly. I mentioned it to Dave and he explained it away by saying he was an intellectual and spent most of his time indoors. Fair enough.

Dave and I chatted, and eventually he made a phone call by which I was approved to join the educational retreat. He drove me through the gates and deposited me in one of the buildings where the orientation was already under way.

I sat in the back of a medium sized room, in a black plastic chair, as our male guide prepared us to meet the guru. He talked about his own experiences, what a rare opportunity this was, etc. There was a huge photo portrait of the guru, about five feet tall, on an easel in the front of the seats. The guru was in his sixties, with long wispy hair, and a very unusual look in his eyes.

At the end of the intro talk, our guide asked if anyone wanted to show respect. A heavy set woman in her fifties walked up the aisle towards the picture and dropped to both knees. Hands up at her sides, palms forward, she fully prostrated herself before her new spiritual master.

I thought, "Oh my. She gave it up so easily."

From there, our group of twenty-five were shuttled around from building to building. We were shown a movie about the guru, then the artwork of the guru, and then some more about the guru. They even led us into a little round room with a thousand pictures of the leader, looking at you from every angle. It was all him, all the time.

Now that we were warmed up and primed, they fed us a light and tasty lunch. While I was in line for it, I overheard one of the residents murmur "Man, I wish the food was like this everyday."

I chatted with a kid in his early twenties, who was anxious to meet the guru, and a mid-thirties gentleman from Germany who had flown over for this very special occasion. There was even a guy in his fifties who had lived on the island in Fiji and served the master directly.

I asked him for some insight on the man and he told me something chilling that I still don't understand.

"What's the guru like?" I asked.

He replied with "Well, it's important to understand that he's not a man."

"What do you mean? He's not a man? He's not an ordinary man, you mean?"

"No," he stated flatly. "I don't know what he is, but he is definitely not a man."

I had read many accounts of people that had sat in meditation with the guru. Some blasted into the psycho-stratospheric heights. People have said he has a primordial awareness, a spiritual personality, much larger than your average man.

I can understand that. It's not that different than a very technical black belt. They may not look that impressive physically, but once you feel what they can do, it seems like magic. But it's just technique and training. It's a technology.

Not everything may be perceived by the eye. Some things must be felt.

The guru had trained under a respected teacher named Rudi, then went to India to see Rudi's teacher, Muktananda.

It seemed to me that he mastered some kind of kundalini yoga as a base skill set. His devotees seemed extremely impressed by his siddha powers. Even integral philosopher Ken Wilber described his spiritual transmission as "industrial strength."

He was a black belt in meditation, and he definitely knew his craft.

The question then becomes what about his students? Was he the kind of teacher who shares it all, who wants his students to surpass his level of understanding? That requires a healthy ego and a vulnerability that has to be constantly renewed.

Or was he the kind of teacher who holds back so that he's the greatest of them all, the lord of his fellowship, the undisputed master?

So far, none of his students had reached the level of his enlightenment. He had copious amounts of materials, books and videos; every kind of media instructive to tell devotees exactly how to live their lives. No shortage of guidance there. So why is it that his students only went so far?

Maybe it was like the world champ whose students never reach his level because he's beating them down so often, then blaming them for failing him. This guru didn't seem like the type to admit his shortcomings as a teacher.

In fact, most of the devotees I had met had a slightly washed out look to them, as if they were being energetically drained. Our tour guide certainly had this look, and at one point he pulled me aside to tell me just how incredible it was to feel the guru living through you, how even his fury was an incredible blessing.

My reservations about this whole experience were growing, even though these people seemed nice enough.

Eventually, our group was heading into darshan, or meditation in the presence of the guru. I could scarcely believe it was happening. That after more than ten years of hearing about this man who's apparently most definitely not a man, I was finally going to see him in the flesh.

Many people were assembled for him at a grassy amphitheater. I chose a spot to sit far away from the stage. From my vantage point, he would be a small blip, but he would also pass by closely as he made his way to his elevated seat.

I was sitting with the old and infirmed, the sick, the people who probably wanted a miracle cure from this god-man. I sat next to a pretty young woman who was caring for her mother with multiple sclerosis. Her mother, unable to move, was flat on the grass while her daughter sat beside her. It was clearly not an easy or insignificant thing for her to be there at that moment.

We chanted, we sang, and we waited and waited. Then we waited some more. Where was this guy?

Eventually, our tour guide let the group know that he wasn't coming. Apparently he didn't feel like it. As I looked around at those wishing to be healed and considered the effort it had required for this girl and her mother to be present, I had my own realization, my own satori. It suddenly became clear that this was not my teacher. This was not my way.

The group went back to a kind of "off campus" building where we were fed fruit and sandwiches. They encouraged us to get our blood sugar back up after that disappointing experience.

At this point, I was noticeably disenfranchised and began pulling away from the group. The group chatter was growing, and I was outnumbered. The stories got more outrageous: now the guru was spiritually responsible for the fall of the Berlin wall and the end of the Cold War. Forget Gorbachev. Forget Reagan. The guru had it handled.

I had to get out of there. I walked out of the room and into a courtyard with nothing but forest beyond it. All I wanted was a touch of separation and some fresh air when an attractive girl approached me and asked if I had any questions or wanted to talk.

I told her I was doing fine by myself. Just wanted to chat on the phone. She let me go and I began dialing numbers.

I reached out to a few people, and the first to answer was Kim. I needed a friendly voice, and she turned out to be the perfect person to talk to.

"You tried it and it didn't work out," she said, giving me some clean cut perspective after such a disappointing spiritual adventure.

Dave picked me up and we got some pizza. He was a good friend. I told him how I was feeling and he said, without judgment, that I simply wasn't ready to meet the guru. I'm sure he was right.

We spent the next day at the hot springs and I flew home in the morning. Back to the real world. Back to my San Diego grind.

I think the wrestlers had it right. It's about self-reliance. Your happiness isn't coming from the outside. It's in you. That's where the power is. That's where your success lies. You can do it yourself.

That's the hard-nosed truth that will protect and propel you, not the blessing of a god-man. It had never been clearer to me.

CHAPTER 11

FALLING OFF
THE PATH

FALLING OFF THE PATH

It can be difficult to put your finger precisely on what's causing dissatisfaction in your life, but you know it's there. After seven years in Southern California, something had shifted inside of me.

San Diego, despite it temperate climate, vast beaches and beautiful women, had become stale. Nothing was as it used to be. The enthusiasm of being in a major metropolitan area with shopping, restaurants, concerts and cultural events, had finally lost its luster.

For a kid raised in Alaska, just being able to survive and thrive in a big city was a vindicating adventure.

But then, one day, the traffic changed from a cool urban experience to a slog that was rotting away my hours on earth. Despite the proximity to the ocean, I wasn't spending time at the beach. I was just hacking it out in a day-to-day existence.

I was surviving, but was I really living?

Things at work had shifted dramatically. Four Square had been the most successful production company in San Diego for decades under the helm of creative director John DeBello. John knew the business and, perhaps even more importantly, he knew how to get the right people for the right positions, to keep the quality level high. I was fortunate enough to be one of those people, but then, suddenly, John was gone.

John and one of the female producers got into a discussion in his office, which took a turn and she walked out on him. John followed her and continued the conversation in a more public area. She decided to file a lawsuit, and John stepped down.

John may have been a bit of a dictator, but he certainly knew what he was doing. The other partner in the company began making some changes, which may have looked good on paper, but were ultimately disastrous for it's long term health.

John's initial replacement didn't have much experience, but she was the partner of one of the DirecTV executives who had given Four Square a lot business.

It was, essentially, a political appointment. A nice woman, to be sure, but after a poor pitch to Seimen's executives, she didn't even bother coming back to work. Eventually, an exceptional man was tapped to become creative director, but at that point it was too late.

Looking back now, it would have been better to bring up one of the people from within the company to helm the ship, as these outside transfers did nothing to bolster our spirits, vision, or bottom line.

I had negotiated my salary through several bumps then hit a ceiling. I rewired and rearranged the studio (with the help of UCSD alum Kent Oberlin), learned basic video editing, took on a series of talented interns from the university, but something was missing. The promise of a bright future was missing for me. I had maxed-out what I could earn and what I could learn.

Several people jumped ship after John's departure, and I was not the last to leave. In the end, the owners stopped showing up and employees had to sell equipment for their final paychecks. A sad demise for a media powerhouse that had dominated the market for so long.

Jiu jitsu had always been there for me though. I had been obsessed with it for years, but everything gets old. Teaching obligations were the only thing that kept me in the game for awhile, Tuesday nights at the Harris Academy, and Sunday mornings at Jiai Aikido.

Brad and I also bought a house together and, with both of us being sharp, urban professionals, we figured we couldn't lose. We bought a compact three-bedroom in an up and coming neighborhood that stretched us both. Timing is everything, and little did we know we'd bought near the top of the market and the peak of the bubble.

Even my relationship with Brad changed. We were still close friends, but we didn't train like we used to. We knew each other's games too well, so training BJJ turned into being workout partners for the squats or pull-ups in the garage. Brad also got deeply into shooting and marksmanship, but personally I didn't find it that interesting.

I had fallen off the pollen path. The path of joy. What was I going to do?

I searched for ways to make it better. I felt that if I just added something, I would be happy again. One more thing to keep my soul from the pain of being out of sync with my calling.

I tried being a youth mentor for a few weeks. I looked into cross training in Aikido, or even going back to Seibukan Jujutsu to work on my next level. I was searching.

I dabbled in a little yoga at the LA Fitness next to work. I'd head there at lunch, and definitely feel better at the end of it.

One of the teachers was quite good. It was more than just a class, it was an experience. She had some students from her main studio attend, and I recall one of the guys being very athletic. He could have done well in jiu jitsu if he wanted, but he chose yoga. Interesting.

I was just about to ask for information about her main studio, when she stopped teaching and some guy replaced her, who treated it like a boot camp workout.

The magic was gone, it was just another club class, and my exploration with yoga would have to wait for a few more years.

Yosemite

The writing was on the wall at Four Square. I was being paid, but the business was opening lines of credit, and it needed some serious new clients to come on board quickly.

The new creative director, John Munoa, actually took a pay cut and reduction in hours to keep me there because he considered me such an essential part of the process, and I thank him for that.

I did some soul searching. My job was good, but not entirely creative. Not like David Helping, Four Square's favorite composer who was actually writing music and getting paid well. That was a dream job. Or was it?

I had been forced to sit, in a very nice chair, but a chair nonetheless, more than forty hours a week for the last four and a half years. The studio space was cool and high tech with the monitors, gear, patch bays and machines, but it didn't have a single window.

It wasn't natural and, after several years of this, I was beginning to feel the effects. I felt out of touch from nature and needed to reconnect in a big way.

I planned a trip to Yosemite National Park with my girlfriend Julie. If you haven't been to Yosemite before, I recommend it.

It is a place of inspiring scale, power and beauty. We stayed in a cabin for a few days and I was able to quiet the other voices, the other minds, the other energies that affect you when you're always surrounded by people.

That trip to Yosemite was a turning point for me. I needed a change. Not just another thing on the schedule. Real change. I needed to quit my job and do something different. Someplace different. I was thirty-one years old. Now was the time.

Did I still want to do audio? What else was there? Well, BJJ seemed like an obvious choice to me. I saw that people from all over the world were flying into see Mr. Harris, many of them running successful academies, and each had escaped the nine to five grind I was deeply embedded in.

Brad and I were like adopted sons to Mr. Harris, and we had received brilliant direct instruction from him over many years, leaving us well qualified to launch a venture of our own.

I could also see that my part time teaching experiment was working. The grappling class at an Aikido studio I led on Sundays was attracting a steady stream of students, from a cool cross section of academies. Whatever mojo I had for attracting people at that point was growing. I couldn't explain it, but I could feel it, and I knew I would be successful if I launched an academy of my own vision.

Where to do it then? I had the opportunity to become partners in Gracie Barra Alaska, or start my own thing. I liked the idea of starting my own thing, and one place I was checking out was Bend, Oregon.

Jimmy is the man who introduced me to Bend. He trained at another academy in San Diego and seriously injured his neck trying to slam his way out of a guillotine. He took an extended period to rehab it and was interested in training again, but only in the right kind of environment. He watched me teach class at the Harris Academy and recognized that I could help create that kind of experience.

He did a series of private lessons with me and, after a few months, I had taken him to a point where he was ready for his blue belt. Mr. Harris tested Jimmy for his first rank and I served as uke. He passed easily.

Jimmy and his wife headed to Oregon, where she had a remote working assignment with her company, and he would take care of the kids. A modern couple with a modern arrangement.

Whenever they were back in town to check in with her company, Jimmy would swing by the Harris Academy and plant the idea of opening a jiu jitsu school in Bend. He said it was an open market. Just a rag-tag group of guys that would roll at a gymnastics academy. Many were dying for a real teacher.

With my all my friends at the Harris Academy, the top post audio seat in San Diego, and a new house purchase with Brad, I swatted down the idea of giving it all up and heading out to some unknown city. Every time. Until I began to feel differently about San Diego.

Then I saw an opportunity, and a possible path.

Recreational Paradise

Bend, Oregon? I had never heard of it before. It was a small town, smack dab in the middle of the state, surrounded by trees and with the Deschutes River running through it. It had been a logging town and a city of twelve thousand or so for most of its existence. But the population began to climb in the eighties and nineties and, after being touted as one the best places to live in several magazines, it had exploded to eighty thousand, with a population geared towards physical fitness and outdoor recreation.

My initial visit was in July, walking into a warm, desert climate and an impossibly blue sky. I stayed with Jimmy and was able to do a seminar at the local gymnastics academy. The seminar was well attended and, during one of the breaks, one of the white belts casually asked what I did off the mat.

I told him that I was a sound designer. His reply was:

"Really? That's what I used to do in LA."

What? Another sound designer in my midst? He introduced himself as Rick Ellis, and little did I know that this man would change my life.

The town was popping with economic activity, and you could smell construction money in the air. Everything seemed to be new. New roads, new housing, new people flowing into the city, including many Californian's who'd sold their homes at the top of the market and were buying into much larger and more comfortable options in Bend.

Jiu jitsu helped me see that my position at Four Square wasn't beneficial anymore. There's a time to hold on to a position, and there's a time to let it go. I was sensitive enough to hold on loosely.

I flew back to San Diego and was confident in my path. I was quitting my job, moving to Bend and launching an Academy.

This was the start of a new life, and I had no idea where it would lead.

The Private Lesson

I decided to compete in the Gracie Worlds before taking my black belt examination.

To help me prepare for the competition, I took a series of private lessons from a young black belt competitor from another gym. The first lesson was great, but during the second one, in a high intensity sparring session, I was injured.

I rolled up for a knee bar, inverted myself, and exposed my right foot in front of his face. He immediately applied a figure four toe hold, hard and fast.

Ping! Ping! Ping!

The tendons in my foot snapped like guitar strings. I'll never forget the sound of it resounding through my body.

I've had many injuries over the years, and I could tell this was bad. In a near fetal position, I reached for my foot as he rolled away.

The first thing out of his mouth was "Damn, I'm never heard anything pop like that. You got weak ankles or something?"

I didn't think I was rolling like an ass, but I could have been. It's possible. Maybe I deserved it. I don't know. I had already tapped several times in the lesson, so I would have gladly tapped to the submission. I just didn't have time.

The instructor asked if I wanted some ice. I told him that would probably help, and he retrieved a small bag with some ice cubes in it from downstairs.

Then, as I iced my rapidly swelling foot, he told me he had some business to take care of at the DMV, and took off.

I limped out of the gym, went home, and took the rest of the day off from work. That night, he sent me an email telling me that I could still compete if I took an Epsom salt bath and wrapped it up tight. It would hurt like hell, but I could do it. I decided to take a pass on this competition. I was watching the signs, and the signs were not good.

I got the foot checked out. I was on crutches for several weeks, went to physical therapy, etc. It was lame.

It took me a long time to forgive that black belt, but I eventually let it go. He isn't a bad guy. Just a beast. It was a moment, and we all have moments. I've had a few myself.

In fact, I chose to look at it as a test of resolve for this new path. Not only was I unable to walk, I contracted a horrible staph infection on my face from their facility.

Which begged the question: did I really want to become a BJJ instructor? A profession where it's likely I'd have more injuries just like this? Most people at my office would never have an injury this severe in their lifetime. As a jiu jitsu professional, not only would these things happen, but I would also have to continue teaching meanwhile.

This was my first chance to truly adapt. I put on my gi and my brown belt and got on the mat with my crutches. I bowed in and taught my Sunday class. It didn't matter. This was happening.

Torn ligaments. Staph infection. Not what I wanted, not what I paid for. But, no matter.

I was going to take Mr. Harris' legendary black belt examination, and I was quitting my job to start an academy. Now, there was no turning back.

CHAPTER 12
BECOMING THE BLACK BELT

悪戦苦闘

BECOMING THE BLACK BELT

One of the Harris Academy members, Phillip Palmejar, had wanted to introduce me to his spiritual teacher for some time.

Her name was Deborah, and she was an early student of Dr. Frederick Lenz.

Dr. Frederick Lenz was a Phd in English Literature, an entrepreneur, and a spiritual teacher. A top student of Sri Chimnoy, a guru noted for his feats of strength and endurance, he eventually went out on his own with a progressive interpretation of Zen Buddhism.

Rama's students were known for being successful professionals and were often into programming.

Dr. Lenz recommended Computer Science as a field of study, aligning the process of programming as similar to Buddhist meditation exercises. His advice was to use your work as a form of spiritual practice, put your all into it, and succeed. There's plenty of success in the world for everyone. Don't hold others back. Do your best, meditate everyday, and you'll get there.

Deborah had led me in a meditation once before, on the cliffs of La Jolla, overlooking the ocean. Now we were going to do another meditation, a group meditation, in the desert. This was a location that her teacher would take groups of students to and, according to generally unreliable eyewitness reports, he would disappear, transform, and manifest powers right in front of them.

I had much lower expectations for the trip. I just wanted to get into the right mental space for the beat down the next day. Looking back, I feel that my black belt exam truly began with that meditation in the Anza Borrego desert.

Phillip picked me up at my house, with a friend in the backseat, and we sped off for the desert.

Phillip took his relationship with Deborah seriously and, since we were running a little behind schedule, he floored it all the way there. No big deal if the road had been a straight shot, but it was long and winding, with treacherous sides carved for fatalities. He was driving so fast that had to ask him to slow it down. "Late is better than dead," I offered.

It was further than I thought, two hours from San Diego, and his vehicle swayed with every turn, threatening to tip.

We arrived. I was still frazzled from the speed of travel. Deborah could sense it and asked if anyone had anything to say. I dropped my anxiety and relaxed into the moment.

As a group, we walked to different areas of the park, heading in the general direction of Font's Point. We would periodically pause, sit down, and meditate. The state park is quite removed, nestled between the population centers, and you can feel the emptiness of the space.

As the sun began to set, we reached Font's Point, a vast expanse of desert looking over the Borrego Valley to the Laguna Mountains. Dramatic. Breathtaking. Jagged and grand. Each group member found a suitable spot to sit quietly and witness the sky change color in a uniquely SoCal sunset.

We meditated until the sun was completely gone and packed up in darkness. Rolling back to San Diego with Phillip and his friend felt markedly different than it had heading out. There was a clarity to our mental state, a relaxed yet energized vibe that had us chatty, thankful and grinning. We hit a Denny's on the way back to San Diego and I went to bed charged. I was ready for the monumental task before me.

The Exam

The Harris black belt exam is an invitation only affair. I had to choose my sparring partners, and sometimes testers will bring smaller or far less skilled players to make the exam less painful and violent. I went the opposite route, choosing my brothers, the guys I trained and rolled with all the time: Brad, Jeff, and Al. This, in and of itself, was a huge factor in determining the difficulty of the test.

I invited one person outside of the crew. Nadija trained with me at the grappling class I led. She was from Sweden and an uchideshi (live in student) at Sunset Cliffs Aikido in Ocean Beach. We never dated, but there was a connection.

Nadija understood the martial artist in me. I had been an uchideshi, she was an uchideshi; I loved BJJ, she loved BJJ; I loved Swedish blonds; she was a Swedish blond. It was perfect. I wanted her there, I knew she'd appreciate the experience.

I picked her up the day of the exam and headed to the Harris Academy. My training partners and I laid out the mats and were warming up when Mr. Harris arrived. I was nervous. Scared, slightly. Jeff's girlfriend Alicia was also on deck, taking photographs.

The brown belt exam had been over two hours, but this was going to be more comprehensive. It had a teaching component, whereas brown belt was more physically grueling and technically oriented. Brad told me my lips had turned blue in the final minutes of that test, so I figured I had that to look forward to at the end of my black belt exam too. If only.

Matt Stansell had already taken the three and a half hour exam. His knee came out three times, but he popped it back in, kept going, and passed. Matt was a stud. He would also dabble in MMA, eventually becoming King of the Cage champion.

Matt was the first black belt. His training partner, lifelong martial artist Jeff Clark, was the second. Kyle was the third, a pressure oriented east coast player who came from the Machado lineage at purple. I was going to be the fourth, but in some ways I was the first truly homegrown Harris black belt who had continued to train at regular group classes after receiving his purple.

The time had come. Mr. Harris strode onto the mat. He asked if I was ready. I assured him that was the case.

We began with side mount escapes. Then mount escapes. We had been going for a few minutes and, to be perfectly honest my body was still warming up, when Jeff got into the mount position and I bridged to escape. But he didn't budge. He locked his hips down hard and I was going to have to put more into it to make this happen.

I bridged explosively. Not quite enough to take him over, but he did move, and our chests separated. His body snapped down as I moved my hand in front of my chest, trying to frame his hips. I heard a pop.

I knew that pop came from me, and that something probably-not-awesome had just happened to my body, but I finished the mount escape anyway. I looked down and saw the tip of my pinky hanging there, like a sad, fleshy chad, and knew this was an imperfect start to an event I had to finish.

Ten minutes in and I'd detached the tendon from the bone in my dominant hand. Whatever. I taped it up to the next finger and soldiered on. This was happening.

The exam was essentially sparring until I was tired, then some kind of teaching challenge. Mr. Harris posited several different kinds:

A first day student who had only seen the UFC; the challenging student who can't stop asking "what if" and "show me the counter" questions; a delinquent class with ADHD that couldn't keep focused; a student with a disability, whether blind, deaf, or with abnormal limbs.

These were things I would face in the real world, only amplified and sometimes comically exaggerated. We laughed during these sections. The delinquent class scenario was downright hilarious.

Then it was back to sparring. Sometimes positional sparring, sometimes goal oriented sparring. Then a little teaching. Then a little more sparring.

What's most important is for Mr. Harris to see you tired. He wants to see your heart. He wants to see how you react when you're under duress and outgunned. So much is revealed when you lose, or are in the process of losing. Many people are gracious in victory, and yet another side is revealed in defeat. Not the pretty side, either.

Mr. Harris rolled with me last. We started from standing and I basically dragged him down I was so tired. He let me try to arm lock him at first, then reversed the situation and put the pressure on.

Make no mistake: it's complete domination. He'd put my arm behind my back and sweep me. He suffocated me with his weight and, when I couldn't go on and was on the verge of breaking, he relented and allowed me to escape and attack.

Then he took the power back again, until I moaned. A moan from deep inside, a moan that sounded wounded and primal. If all singing is crying, then all moaning is dying. It's the sounds of your spirit rising up to defend you when there's nothing more to give.

Finally, after what seemed like an eternity, it all stopped. I was totally and completely exhausted. Empty. Hours of exertion had come to a halt.

A stillness overtook me. I was simply there. Buzzing in the moment. Buzzing in the now. Inhale. Exhale.

There was stillness, and the realization that I had done it.

All of us, my training partners and Mr. Harris, sat in a circle and discussed the exam. What I did well on, what needed improvement. For this test, my standup was a weak spot. With my ankle still injured, I had a reason to be rusty, but it was an indication that Mr. Harris was taking a look at everything closely. This was not the end. Nor was it just a whipping. It was a carefully measured rite of passage that signaled the beginning of serious study.

We stood up and by this time there were some people rolling in for the JKD class.

Mr. Harris announced that we had a new black belt in our midst. Standing behind me, he untied my brown belt and placed it on my shoulder.

He wrapped the black belt around my waist.

I looked at my training partners, who had help to make this happen. I almost broke down when I looked at Brad, my brother who had walked this path beside me.

People in attendance applauded and I said a few words, thanking my teacher, and sharing a little bit of what this meant to me. It meant so much more than I could express in that moment, but the sentiments were somehow transmitted.

I drove Nadija back to Ocean Beach. It was the last time I would see her, and she kissed me on the cheek as she said goodbye.

I drove to a random Mexican restaurant, ordered two full dinners for myself, and went back to the house. Al rolled over and we celebrated with a drink and a smoke.

I will never forget climbing into the shower that evening, with my swollen ankle and my finger hanging sadly, and feeling the deepest ache I've even known, past my muscles, and down into my bones.

I had never felt so alive.

Launching A Vision

I had no idea what was in store for me going forward. But I had a feeling that, if I put my all into it and pumped it with enough love, it would be successful. That's the way it had worked so far, and I was determined to continue that trend.

Yes, I would be teaching jiu jitsu, but I was going to do it differently. Think differently. I was going to put the art in the best light possible, leveraging skills from all areas of my life, especially my media experience.

I didn't know how I was going to do it, but I was doing it. I heard that fortune favors the bold, and doors would open unexpectedly. I trusted in that. I could figure out the rest along the way.

That college degree gave me that confidence that I could teach myself. I was leaving San Diego with a degree, professional experience, and high level martial arts skills. Not bad.

Many people have told me I have beautiful jiu jitsu, but I knew that alone wouldn't be enough to make it. Even a world championship is not enough. There are unbelievably tough guys out there that are broke and just struggling to survive.

That would not be my fate. I was going to leave the nine to five grind, not look back, and make a contribution to this discipline that had changed my life.

Jiu jitsu is not just movement patterns and physics, it's an art. It needed to be represented as such.

I had a vision. I wanted to share that vision.

I hoped people would respond to it positively.

But I had no idea how my life would change.

CHAPTER 13
ART OF
THE ACADEMY

RENSHI

INSTRUCTOR

ART OF THE ACADEMY

I didn't have any money when I started the Academy. But I had a vision, a few good friends, and the willingness to work hard. It was enough.

Julie and I arrived in Bend in October. It was a crisp morning. As the sun rose, we peered out of the window to survey the view for the first time. Frosted treetops greeted us as the elevation dropped below our vantage point. It was a nice spot.

It was a long drive from San Diego, with an overnight in Redding, California, and I was in an entirely new environment. The next step in my journey had just gotten a lot more real.

I had rented a room from a cool older gentleman named JJ. The rental market in Bend was red hot, even though I couldn't move up right away to take the room, he held it for me, and cancelled on another potential roommate.

Why? He heard the passion in my voice, and knew I'd be the right fit. He knew that I was going to make it. That I would be successful. He could hear I was hungry. He had me pay September's rent even though I wouldn't be there until the next month, and I'm glad I did. The right fit is well worth it.

The house was almost empty when my girlfriend and I arrived. JJ was still living and working in Seattle, so I agreed to pick up various pieces of furniture to get the house set up. Almost every item had been purchased through Craigslist. JJ was a black belt bargain hunter to the core. He knew how to leverage money.

As a man, I can survive in a spartan environment, but there's no denying a woman's touch elevates the house to a home. Julie helped me to get the place set up, and I had the good fortune of sharing with a week with her before she went back to San Diego. Even though she didn't quit her job to move up with me on this new adventure, we were going to stay in touch.

On her last night in town I realized that we still hadn't come up with a logo for the academy. As my chief graphic designer, she presented a grid of several dozen circular options, but I wasn't really digging any of them. Nothing resonated. Nothing jumped. Most of them too complicated for my taste.

I needed something more basic. Something timeless. Something modeled after a traditional Japanese family crest, or moen.

We started fresh. Just a circle. Then we placed three smaller sized circles of equal size inside of it, implying the shape of a triangle, representing mind, body, and spirit. A smaller circle was placed in the center, and a thin ring placed around the outside. It looked distinct. Simple. Timeless.

My new family crest was finished in under twenty minutes. When the creativity is flowing, there's no holding back.

This was my lesson in branding. My first real step. Initially, I thought that setting up your own martial arts school was about teaching. About giving. It is, but there's so much more than that.

It's about branding. It's about business. It's about leading.

It's about being calm and professional in a discipline that's ripe with passion and excitement.

It's about making a difference on whatever scale you can, by putting your heart into each step, so the beneficial ripples can be felt far and wide.

Overcoming Fear

I have to be honest: I was scared. I had just quit my job that I had labored to get after a tough university run. I felt relatively alone. I knew Jimmy, and I now I knew Rick. I talked to my friends back in San Diego but, overall, there was a sense of isolation in this new environment, particularly by moving there at the beginning of winter. Which, for a budding entrepreneur, is not necessarily a bad thing.

Having worked the nine to five grind in San Diego for the last four and a half years, I had some difficulty adjusting to the slowdown; to the pace of the town and the pace of my days. Bend is a little bit sleepy.

I was three weeks out from starting classes in a new city and I didn't have a clue how to run a business. I had worked for them, some good, some bad, but had never run one.

But I was dedicated, willing to learn, and determined to succeed.

On a deeper level, I felt a calling to do this. If I had spent the hours of my youth in a more religious environment I would have started a church with the level of passion that I felt. I was a different kind of preacher, on a matted pulpit, broadcasting a vision of hope and personal transformation.

It's as if a voice inside of me had laid it out: "You've been training your entire life for this. Now is the time. Do something great."

Books were the first place to start. 'Think And Grow Rich' is the classic guide. 'The E-Myth', 'Rules for Revolutionaries', and 'The Four Hour Work Week' were also instrumental.

Rick was a mentor for this budding businessman, and we became fast friends. We would hang out and talk about business, partly as brainstorming for this academy he was helping to build, and partly as therapy for me to alleviate my stress levels over becoming an entrepreneur.

He was doing well with his software company, Expression Engine, which had become the designer's choice as a content managing system (CMS) on websites. This was partly due to its customizability, and partly because of its airtight security.

Rick felt like an older brother by about ten years. Here was a fellow musician and sound designer who had escaped the nine to five grind. He knew how to do it, and I wanted to learn that skill too. Jiu jitsu was going to be my vehicle to freedom.

Rick, and his belief in me, would change my life forever. He was an artist in his own right, but also a producer, and I was the talent in this production.

There was a lot to learn: articles of incorporation, guerrilla marketing, advertising, payments, patches and clothing. The list is endless and evolving. I needed to get familiar and learn some new business skills. The uncertainly of it all kept me on my toes.

Blogging was just getting started, and the academy blog, as well as the website Rick designed, was something people found inspiring.

Visually, it was light years ahead of the competition. But maybe it's also how fresh my perspective was because of the vulnerability I displayed through my words. I was introspective. Honest. Discovering who I was, in this new role. One post at a time.

From the Blog: Appetites Change

I find it hard to train sometimes. Hard to train in certain arts. Brazilian Jiu Jitsu is difficult to come back from, once you've gotten a taste of it.

Aikido is an art I still love and revere, and one I trained seriously in. I read every book. A kind of a devotee. But now it's just difficult. Same with Seibukan Jujutsu. Fun for a couple of days, but hard to really get into for a long period of time.

Let's cut to the chase. There's no sparring in those arts. That's what it comes down to. No REAL sparring.

There's randori in aikido, which has one person attacked by (generally) three partners at once. But the attacks are too often a double handed grab and a telegraphed shomen strike. It's more of a high intensity movement exercise, very fast paced, with very little contact. Good aikido feels like just missing your target.

Seibukan Jujutsu is a little better. Henka is the name of their sparring equivalent. Attacks have a bit more variation, whether they're strikes or grabs, and the techniques allow for some creativity. Atemi is light. Cooperation, to some degree, is expected. They are beautiful dances and, at one time, were fully satisfying, but my appetite has changed. I'm now a meat eater.

Graduated training is important. Kata, technical exercises, jiyu waza (medium paced flowing variations), then henka or randori. But these other arts stop before the randori (sparring) of Judo and Brazilian Jiu-Jitsu. The full resistance. It can be crushing to the ego when your pressure tested skills and rank do not match. But when they do, it brings real confidence. And if you tap someone easily, when they least expect it, against their best efforts, you trigger an awakening in them. I've seen it many times. The person's eyes light up, and they say "Whoa, that was cool." There's real wonder and awe. Whatever that was, they'd like to be able to do it.

I felt that way the first time I sparred in Judo, with my high school team captain, Ichikawa. I got a first class ticket on the Uchimata Express. But I was hooked. Whatever that was, I wanted to learn how to do it too. And I'm still at it.

Birth of an Academy

November was the birth of the Academy. A truly modest beginning. I began teaching out of a local Karate studio in the evening hours, after their regular classes. Rick, Jimmy, and a judo champion named Nathan, were on the mat for those early sessions.

I was still nursing that little finger on the right hand. My ankle was basically healed, but the pinkie wasn't good. The tip drooped, it looked sad, and didn't feel strong enough to grip with. I protected it with a cheap drug store splint, and hoped for the best, using my willpower and discipline to not spar until my finger was ready for action.

Two weeks into classes, and eight weeks since the injury, I was dying to spar. I knew Nathan had great control, so I asked him to roll. Less than a minute in, I gripped his gi and felt a pop. My little finger began to swell.

I severed that graft without significant effort and the last two months of healing were down the drain. Not good. I bowed out from the roll immediately and got changed.

I needed to see a specialist. My pinky was jacked and so was my neck. I needed to get my body back in order so I could perform for my students.

I went to a hand doctor and he knew exactly what was going on: mallet finger. It often happens when people spill something on the carpet and, while vigorously rubbing it out, they catch their finger and pop the tendon from the bone. Not that uncommon.

The solution was to tape it absolutely flat to a splint and keep it in that position for three months, non stop. Every waking moment, including in the shower, I had to protect that finger if I wanted a strong graft.

The mindfulness I held for that little finger had never been greater, but I was frustrated. I wanted to show how good I was. Everything I could do. I wanted to showcase the art. But I had to be patient. It was not my time.

Jimmy was my first student, and Rick the second. A small group began to form around me, with quite an age range. It wasn't just the young bucks. I was teaching them slowly, setting them up for later success, laying a foundation of fundamental movements and positional escapes in every class.

How do you create an academy from scratch? I believe it starts with ukemi, or falling skills. The ability to shoulder roll and fall to the ground safely. To protect yourself in the most fundamental way.

Many people start out in martial arts anxious to apply their techniques against someone, when the most important thing, the most fundamental skill, is actually the ability to move yourself. Your strength can be magnified, and leverage optimized, if you're in the right position.

Position yourself wisely, and external control is so much easier. A small shift can make all the difference.

This is art of jiu jitsu.

From the Blog: The Most Important Thing

I had a private lesson with a new student on Saturday. TJ has a background in Aikido, and wanted to take the private as a general preparatory overview for class. Having trained with Chiba Sensei in San Diego for several years, his ukemi was excellent and he was already way ahead of the curve. I went over more movement exercises, showing him how to round out your body and be a ball, rather than a block, to overcome the friction of the ground.

Then I showed him more conceptual aspects of BJJ: a straight arm lock from the guard (which he did very nicely), followed by a little exposition on mechanics, how important they were, and how blocking critical mechanics are the key to reversals. Then we linked triangle with arm lock, so he could see how one attack leads to another, to act as the distraction and off balance your opponent, putting them one step behind. I also covered "empty corners" in a sweep from the arm lock, so TJ could feel how much easier it is to direct your energy where your partner has no base.

Finally, we covered variations of escaping side mount, tying it together with the fundamental movement of Brazilian Jiu Jitsu, the snake move. TJ asked what he should be focusing on most intently. I recommended focusing on basics and positional escapes. And as I've thought about it more, I can put it even more succinctly:

Students should always be focused on how to move themselves, not their partner. Learn to control your body, your movements, your timing, and not only will it become more difficult for others to control you, you will be better able to control them. It begins with self-control.

Local Rivalries

The Academy was growing, and I was doing every kind of advertising available, from business cards in coffee shops to ads in the free weekly paper. Rick recommended putting "Bend's Only Black Belt in Brazilian Jiu Jitsu" in the ad, so I did.

It seems that caught the attention of a local brown belt, who took umbrage at this bold statement of fact. He trained under the highly respected godfather of BJJ in the Pacific Northwest, Marcelo Alonso, and called me up on a placid afternoon.

"Hello. This is Roy Dean"

"Roy Dean, this is JT Taylor."

"JT, how are you?"

"Good. I just wanted to call you up and let you know that you're not the only black belt in Bend anymore. I got my black belt certificate and you can come by anytime if you want to take a look at it."

"Dude, congratulations. I know what a long journey it is. That's fantastic. I don't need to take a look at the certificate. I believe you."

So that was our first conversation. Pretty cordial. Then he sent me some weird on-line messages. So I called him up to talk about it, and work through it in a brotherly manner.

It rapidly devolved to an invitation to fight him in a variety of situations: including, but not limited to, in the streets or on the mat, with or without a shirt. There was even an offer to fight with a sword at one point, but I feel that was just the warrior in him waxing philosophically.

JT made it clear that he wasn't afraid of me. In truth, I had a lot of respect for his skills. He was a good fighter, in jiu jitsu and MMA. But I had no interest in small town rivalries. The scale of my vision was much grander.

Plus, tactically speaking, I would never give him what he wanted. It's more fun to torture him with desire. Even if I accepted, trained, and got on the mat, it was possible our friend could have gone missing and not shown up for the match. That had happened before. Several times, actually.

JT didn't show for an MMA match with Matt Lindland, and then drove to Portland to challenge Matt at Team Quest one week before he was fighting in the UFC.

The timing was ridiculous. Matt grabbed a phone book and suggested that JT get some counseling.

My modus operandi with difficult people is to step around them and, if they're unstable, then keep them at arms length. Assist them if you can, of course, by skillful means. That's the Buddhist way, but don't get sucked into their drama.

Not everyone operates within a rational framework. I've learned this the hard way, more than once.

I had a weird housing situation back in my college days, with a questionable roommate. He was unusually aggressive and, although things were tense and even got close to becoming physical, I kept my cool and never engaged. I moved out soon after.

The guy who took my place was then selected for harassment. That was a mistake. The new roommate beat Mr. Aggression down, fists powered by divine justice, and he wasn't even trained.

The moral of the story was: the universe took care of it. Keep moving. Don't engage with the unstable, no matter how loudly they cry out for a fight.

Things calmed down with JT, then flared up with some threats against my clients several months later. JT relayed to me in writing that his students were going to break the arms and legs of my clients in the next tournament. Typical Cobra Kai stuff.

This disturbed me. There's a level of amusement in threats against myself. But my students are an entirely different matter.

What should my tolerance policy be with threats against clients? Zero tolerance?

My line of thinking was that my students were my responsibility. Their development and safety are an integral part of my own development as a teacher. I was not going to lead them into a dangerous situation, on the mat or on the road, when the deck is stacked against them.

If students came home with broken arms or ankles, and the scenario had been forewarned and whispered to me, I would have felt partially responsible. We don't need a sweep the leg situation. What if Miyagi had been warned by Kreese? It colors everything.

There were professional and legal issues at hand, so I sought a second opinion.

I ran this by one of the trusted men of the dojo, Darryl. Darryl is an accomplished surfer, rock climber, and skier. A total badass under wraps. Understated, as I like all my heroes to be. He loved jiu jitsu and was also working for the District Attorney.

Darryl read the correspondence, and it qualified for deeper investigation. I ended up giving Grand Jury testimony on the case and, though charges weren't pressed, it was held on his record for a few years. He was also told by law enforcement, in a kind and courteous manner, to not contact me again. JT, ever the gentleman, complied.

So that's how I was going to handle this business, and all my business. Professionally. Through the proper channels. No junior high school drama.

I have a low tolerance for bullies, but now the protocol for dealing with them had been codified, and the vision for the Academy was clear.

Roy Dean Academy was going to be the Mercedes Benz of Brazilian Jiu

Jitsu. Professional. High minded. Respectful, with a nod to tradition. Open source, with a progressive approach; fueling the evolution of the art.

This was my vision, and it was just getting off the ground. Even more, I realized that I had become the responsible adult in the room, leading other adults into an unknown realm.

I took the responsibility seriously. I was all grown up.

CHAPTER 14

MEDIA REVOLUTION

MEDIA REVOLUTION

I promised myself to stay out of the nine to five grind.

Even though the Academy wasn't initially profitable, I felt that, if I ended up taking a side job, I'd be splitting my focus and, ultimately, less successful.

I had to keep moving forward toward a scalable, profitable version of my business.

Rick urged me to approach the business differently from the beginning. Yes, I'd have the Academy, and I understood that a comfortable living could be made with the right number of students, but that also had inherent limitations.

Bend is a small town, and it won't yield the same kind of numbers a major metropolitan area does. Small town, small market.

What I really wanted was a profitable online business, in addition to my academy, where I could focus on transmitting the art in a very specific way, and develop a global footprint.

I heard whispers that the Crossfit Journal had ten thousand subscribers, at $25 a year. No distribution costs, or time delays, and many articles were submitted by the readership.

I liked that business model. The math was certainly appealing, and I've always been a decent writer. Plus, I was deeply knowledgable about jiu jitsu, with connections to high level practitioners in Japanese Jujutsu, BJJ, Aikido, and more.

My idea was to create a quarterly publication titled "The E Journal of Jujutsu", or EJJ. Multiple styles of jujutsu would be included, and the presentation would be artsy. Julie helped me with the layout, and I reached out to a few friends for articles, in addition to creating content myself.

My friend Alicia provided most of the photos. Brad introduced me to Robb

Wolf, a biochemist he met at the first Crossfit certification, who had an online magazine called Performance Menu. We wrote content for one another, so Performance Menu had some functional grappling guidance, and the EJJ had conditioning recommendations.

Rick set me up with a web developer to get a subscription module going online, and though it was expensive, I looked at it as an investment. I poured money and time into the EJJ, but after nine months it still wasn't catching on. Demand for that kind of information was already being sated by online forums for free, and in a more timely manner. It just wasn't the right model for that kind of information.

Heading into my fourth issue, Robb told me that he was getting out of the game and selling the magazine to his friend Greg Everett. That was the final sign that the EJJ had to go. It wasn't working and I wasn't enjoying it. Rob was focusing all of his energy on writing his book "The Paleo Solution" which went on to great success in the marketplace. I needed a new focus too.

Maybe DVDs were the answer. Mr. Harris had several successful titles in the marketplace, including the popular "BJJ 101" series (which started off with a conceptual approach to the use of space and weight I had never heard before. Clearly this man knew more than just techniques and was a very special instructor).

Brad and I participated in many DVD filming sessions after class at the Harris Academy, including the highly influential DVD "BJJ Over 40". Mr. Harris proved, once again, with that title and it's popularity, that he was a man ahead of his time.

I was comfortable on camera. No performance anxiety. I had seen it done with DirecTV sports this week, and I knew that it was now my time to be the on-air talent.

BJJ Seminars Year One was the first project, and it was a markedly different from anything else on the market. It contained two black belt seminars, one from myself and one from Mr. Harris, Jimmy's purple belt demonstration, a highlight version of a summer seminar, and a commercial I filmed just before leaving Four Square, titled "What Does Jiu Jitsu Look Like?"

That disc served as a soft introduction to my personal presentation and jiu jitsu style, and some people loved it. It sold, but it was hardly a home run.

I sent a copy of it to perhaps the greatest pound for pound grappler of all time, Marcelo Garcia. He was kind enough to offer this response.

> *Hi Roy,*
>
> *I have just finished watching your DVD. I found the way you teach is very detail oriented, which is a great quality in an instructor. I also enjoyed watching the way you sparred with people in seminars, especially with the kids. Overall, I would recommend your DVD and wish you the best of luck!*

I had the blessing of MG. Nothing could stand in my way.

Keith Owen was also a fresh black belt under esteemed Professor Pedro Sauer and had recently released his first DVD. We supported each other in the launch of our titles, and it was good to have a new friend, from a different lineage, with similar ambitions for spreading the art.

The next instructional was more straightforward. It was called Brazilian Jiu Jitsu Blue Belt Requirements. Essentially, I would demonstrate and explain Mr. Harris' belt requirements, which he had spelled out clearly for students seeking rank under him from around the world.

His focus from white to blue was on positional escapes, and developing skilled movements in bridging and shrimping. There were submissions, but proficiency using those submissions against resisting opponents wasn't required. It was a thoughtful and efficient selection of techniques and movements that would lay a strategic groundwork for the student's development.

Rick filmed a few sections, but there were some audio issues with the overhead lights that made me deem the whole thing unusable for a DVD. So I uploaded the videos to YouTube and gave them away. The power of free was revealed to me in short order. People loved them, and nobody ever complained about the audio.

The aesthetic in Blue Belt Requirements was simple. I wore a blue gi, on traditional green tatami mats spilling out behind me, with weapon racks on the far back wall. The audio was clear, we had real lighting, and the entire thing was tightly edited and neatly chaptered. Two DVDs of material with no filler.

I edited in iMovie, authored with iDVD, and had it replicated in San Francisco. Julie did the sleeve design and disc art. Very professional, with a corporate influence. Non-violent cover imagery. The thoughtfulness of the DVD set resonated with people around the world, and I can honestly say that Blue Belt Requirements changed my life.

It's exciting having a successful product, a successful part of you, in the marketplace. I was dealing in shiny discs, delivered in little white boxes. In the beginning, I'd handwrite each address. Eventually I printed labels, which I'd place on the box in perfect alignment. Every detailed mattered.

Before printing postage could happen from a desktop, I made many trips to the post office, and was a slave to their 5:15pm deadline. International shipments required specific stamps and paperwork. I was grateful to be making money, but being chained to the post office was not ideal.

Blue Belt Requirements showed techniques and movements necessary for the first graded level at my academy, but also gave a glimpse beyond with technique combinations. Also included were three blue belt demonstrations, with the participants roughly a decade apart in age, one each in their twenties, thirties, and forties.

The demonstrations had a minimalist framework: static demonstration of techniques against a non-resistant opponent, followed by four rounds of sparring. The expected and the unknown. The pre-determined and spontaneous. This format is heavily influenced by Seibukan Jujutsu.

The sparring partners in "The Murder Squad" were chosen in the moment, but also with great consideration, based on who was there, how their games matched up, how much energy the demonstrator still had, etc.

Unless I was injured, I was always the last round. I would submit them, but also allow them to submit me to finish the demo. They had to slay the master. They would be pushed, and the tougher they were, the harder and farther they were pushed.

Then I'd allow an opening, a sudden reversal of fortune, so, if their eyes were still open and they were still mentally in the game, they could capitalize on the opening and submit me for the finale.

It was a glorious ritual for viewers and participants alike.

The titling convention for these videos was simple: the students' last name, followed by the belt level. For example, Rick Ellis getting his purple belt would be Ellis Purple.

I created a bit of a monster for myself with these demonstrations. Jimmy's purple belt demo was the first. Rick's was the first blue belt demo. Many others followed.

It was storytelling, it was conflict, it was a carefully controlled struggle where the person would emerge victorious and the viewer could share in that victory. They could also observe the development of my academy and students from the comfort of their homes. Filming my academy had become a long-term art project.

Almost all of my students elected to participate in this rite of passage. Putting these demos up for all the world to see was considered a controversial step in an art which prized sport competition as the chief gateway to the next rank. It was different, and anything different invites both criticism and praise.

The demonstrations were definitely creating a buzz, through the comments section under the videos on YouTube, and in online forums as well. I stepped in to clarify before misconceptions took hold, as they often do with the online populace.

From the Web: On Belt Testing in BJJ

Many people find the subject of belt testing in Brazilian Jiu Jitsu controversial.

My personal approach is this. Although I give the student the option of doing a public demonstration, or "test", I do not charge for them. Every student that does a demonstration is already at the level they are testing for. It is not a stretch. I have already deemed them worthy, through close observation, and personally feeling their technique.

I will present them with their belt in class if they don't want the public display. The "test" is a chance for them to experience a rite of passage, a goal that they've geared their training towards, an event that they can share with their friends and family, on and off the mat. The demonstration is an optional activity, and is a way of creating an experience that enhances your training. Just like a tournament, your focus on training changes leading up to the event. The blade is gradually honed.

Competition is one way of testing your skills and is an important accelerator for those that are serious about training in the art. It will alert you to holes in your game like nothing else, and I have personally benefitted from competition. Competitions are an important component of training, but they are only a portion of the whole. They can be a great experience, or a horrible extension of the art. I have been to many a terrible tournament running hours behind schedule, with absent minded officials and inadequate facilities.

Some of these competitions are expensive to travel to, costly to enter, and may only give you a five minute experience of what you've trained years to learn how to do. Your opponent may get two points for a takedown and stall for the win. You may only have to win one match in your division for the gold medal. Or, if you're a middleweight blue belt, it's likely you'll fight four or five times before clinching a medal. The quality of experience can vary dramatically.

These demonstrations are a way of creating a sustained martial experience. I work my students during the test. Not everything is shown in the condensed video versions. Blue belt exams are about forty-five minutes. The purple is over an hour.

I chose to edit out the part of Jimmy dry heaving on the mat as Mr. Harris applied pressure, or the people lifting him to his feet after it was over. That's part of it, but the pain isn't appealing to everyone, and I really want these videos to inspire people to train, not create an aversion to the art by fear of suffering. Spouses have felt uncomfortable, and even shed a tear in my dojo, watching their loved one suffer in side mount. I take them to a very controlled point of exhaustion, appropriate for their age and physical condition.

Under Mr. Harris, the tests definitely get more intense as the belt gets darker. My brown belt was rough. The black was a crucifixion. Three and a half hours of sparring, teaching, and technical demonstration. Exhaustion beyond belief. Pressure. Exhilaration. Emotion. Few people will ever go through that kind of crucible in their lives, requiring such a high level mix of skill, athleticism, and heart.

It took me six months to fully heal from the exam, and I certainly would never inflict something like that on my new students. That will come later. It takes years to build up to something like that. That test, for me, was the culmination of fifteen years of dedicated martial training. A one year blue belt should not have to take the full monty.

A blue belt demonstration should temper the spirit, not break it. Twist it, turn it, torture it a little, but leave it intact so that it can grow stronger. And it will. The techniques you've programmed into your body are good. Positional escapes are emphasized, laying the foundation of a solid BJJ game. Takedowns and headlock escapes are also required, plus basic submissions.

This is machine code: low level programming that is not particularly powerful in and of itself, but really turns into something amazing once higher level programming languages (concepts, combinations, tactics and strategy) build upon it. But the machine must be programmed first.

In the blue belt demonstration, students show that they can execute the techniques with very little power. This is how trained eyes will measure a performance. Do they have the angles worked out, and where are their knees, hands, and feet placed? Are they smooth in their movement, or are they stuttering and second-guessing themselves?

You have to be smooth and confident to get a submission in a small window of opportunity against an actively resisting opponent. You have to have the angles worked out, and not rely on power, when you go against a much stronger or larger opponent. The question is: how little energy can you use to get the job done?

After the technical portion, we get live. Twenty minutes of sparring for the blue belt. That's the equivalent of four competition matches. Against blue belts and above. It's not easy with all eyes on you. But the most meaningful accomplishments are never easy.

It's not what you do, it's how you do it. In martial arts and in life. Anyone can punch, it's how you punch that matters. The mechanics of a choke are not difficult, but figuring out how to enter into it, against all body types, martial backgrounds, and levels of intent, is the path to mastery. A test can sell an art short, or it can be a transformational experience for those watching, and the person participating.

It's all in how you do it.

CHAPTER 15
THIRD STREET DOJO

BOUKEN

ADVENTURE

THIRD STREET DOJO

"Hey Roy. Do you know of anyone that would be willing to sublet my dojo?"

"I think I do."

"Who are you thinking of?"

"Me."

Brian just renewed the lease at his dojo, but after examining projections for their continued growth, he and his wife knew they had to move. They found another space, after signing this lease, and were looking for a way out.

The location he was leaving behind had a long history as a martial arts school, teaching Kempo for many years, before being home to Brian and his Shotokan inspired style.

There were aspects of this space that were highly desirable. It would be my own spot. The mat frame was already in place. It was on a heavily trafficked road. Many saw Third Street as a dividing line between the two sides of town.

Bendite's are all about which side of town you live on. The Westside is more trendy, upscale, and expensive. It's also more beautifully wooded. The Eastside is still good, but perceived as more blue-collar.

This space was essentially a turnkey operation. It had recently been renovated with the lease renewal, with three small dressing rooms in the back, an office and a mat frame that was ready to be filled. I didn't have the cash for new mats, so I worked a deal where I could use the mats from an Aikido club in exchange for a sublet. Now all it needed was some paint, and I'd be in business.

I was so ready for my own spot. It had been a winding road to get there. We started in a less functional version of this dojo, then we sublet from a large

Aikido school. Six months later, as their lease expired, we all shared space with another Aikido academy.

Although there wasn't a ton of interaction between the two groups, the Aikido and BJJ folks got along well. The two Aikido groups didn't gel, though. Two different teachers, two different styles. Too closely related. Shiite and Sunni Muslims, basically.

The space was far from perfect, but it was perfect for me. It had mountain views from the second story, yes, but there was also a fast food sign intruding on the sunsets. Occasionally homeless folks would sleep up on the roof and I'd gently nudge them on their way before class started on Saturday mornings

My opening move was to transform Brian's red, white and blue motif into something a little subtler. I chose a beige palette, with a dark brown accent wall, which complimented the cool green mats. We organized a paint and pizza party with academy members and everyone pitched in. We were putting our personal stamp on the place.

At one point, Rick looked directly at me, paintbrush in hand, and said:

"Mr. Dean, you've arrived."

There was no denying it. I had. The dream was coming true and I was finally in my own spot. With my own aesthetic. Now that I had a permanent location and a dedicated facility, more things began falling into alignment. This included attracting a number of long distance students.

A British Tae Kwon Do champion named Steven Greenaway was the first. He was sent a video of Jimmy's purple belt demonstration by a friend, and was suitably intrigued.

That's the kind of BJJ he wanted to learn.

Not the fight-for-your-survival and almost-get-your-arm-broken-every-class kind of BJJ that he had available in his area. He wanted to learn the art in a more accessible way and create an environment that would foster his own development, along with the development of others.

Steve called me up from England and asked about becoming a long distance student and affiliate. We had a great rapport and he booked a trip for himself, his girlfriend Kirsty, training partner Paul, and a gentleman named Adam, to train with me in Bend.

They arrived at the dojo just as the mats were being laid down for the first time. Prescient timing, to be sure. Other good people would follow suit over the years as affiliates, and I did my best to assist them on their BJJ journey, during every step that they were with me, whether it was short term or long.

Things were coming together professionally, but unraveling at home. Julie had left her place in San Diego and moved in with me. I proposed to her at Crater Lake National Park on a sunny day, freshly fallen snow on the ground, in storybook conditions. We were both highly optimistic.

Over time, we both realized the move to Bend wasn't working for her. Her design business wasn't taking off at the rate she would have liked. She wasn't making friends. She was a big city girl now living in a very small town. The city had some high end features, but also some backward aspects. It's gentrification was not complete.

It wasn't the right fit for her. It certainly wasn't the way I imagined it was going to be, and the reality didn't seem tenable. We still loved each other, and mutually agreed that calling off an engagement was better than a divorce.

"Watch the signs," the great jujutsu master Yasuhiro Irie once told me. I paid attention and they weren't telling me to move forward.

I saw myself at a crossroads. I was heading to Kuwait for a seminar and that journey would not only be a new experience, but it represented an entirely new path. A path that could deliver a unique and unconventional life, but such arrangements come at a price. There's always a price to pay.

I chose the path less traveled. The path of adventure.

Kuwait shifted my perspective dramatically. It was the most fascinating intersection of sand, steel, and glass. Traditional garb and ultra modern amenities. A cocktail of cultures, stirred quickly, swirling and colliding.

My host, Ahmed Alhouli, was great, and someone I recognized as a tribal leader. He was a brother from another mother, a brother from another land.

Ahmed traveled to Brazil in his twenties, took the heroes journey to learn BJJ and then brought that fire back to Kuwait, just as I had taken it to Bend. A black belt under the legendary Draculino, he also has a background in classical Japanese jujutsu. We related on many levels.

The food in the Middle East is out of this world. Fresh hummus, grilled meats and avocado-mango smoothies I still dream about. There was a chicken and rice dish delivered on a cardboard flat that could be a daily staple. I'm a bit of a foodie and I was duly impressed.

Every time I visit Kuwait, there is an effort to on their part to share the Islamic faith, which I sincerely appreciate.

I am a guest in their country, listening and asking questions on a subject that is far beyond dear to their hearts. It is the over-arching soul of their social structure.

When I sat down for a lecture at the Islamic Outreach Center, my guide began, "We are in the middle of a cosmic battle between good and evil. This is a fact."

I simply nodded.

The fact that he would declare that as a fact is all I needed to know. Self contained certainty. A useful tool, which often feels good, but can be misused and misapplied.

I appreciated the thoughtfulness of sharing their faith, a faith that they honestly believed would improve my daily life. How can you fault people for trying to help you?

As long as you don't have to accept that help or face the sword, then we're good.

Islam really does bring people together in a humble and heartfelt way. The simple act of giving up to the Other can be powerful and transformative. The understanding that there are forces greater than yourself, which you must yield to in order to create harmony in your life, is immensely relieving. Jiu jitsu can also teach you this. How to blend. Let go. Unclench your fist. Release the grip.

We long for this.

Hearing the prayer call go out in the morning over the city's loudspeaker was an exotic treat I relished, then I slept deeply into the afternoon with the time zone inversion. I toured several mosques and fell in love with Middle Eastern architecture. What stunning monuments we make as men to celebrate the mystery of it all.

Religions are technologies that allow man to relate to the divine. But technologies change. The needs of societies change. Change is the rule in this realm, and occasionally updates are needed.

Christianity has had its reformations and evolutions, often dragging its feet, to put it mildly. But it has evolved, for better and for worse. Islam is young in this regard.

Holy books are useful, but we should trust our own intelligence and experience to recognize what's antiquated, what's oppressive, and what doesn't honor modern human rights. It's not that hard to overcome the dissonance.

Our Muslim friends must accept that the Quaran is not the infallible word of God, just as the old and new testaments were not actually penned by Jehovah's hand. Divinely inspired, I'll give you. But infallible? The evidence suggests otherwise.

You might as well say invincible. This kind of religious devotion is found in martial arts too. Of course. The master was invincible. Untouchable. Capable of killing without contact.

MMA helped dispel a lot of these myths in martial arts, through the crucible of experimentation. Maybe we need a similar arena for religious belief, and we'll see that the cross-trained do better than the specialists.

We have to allow variation and evolution in these religious technologies that serve us, or we will end of serving them. It's that certainly of being right that fuels the fascists of every era. In every argument.

The invitation to teach a seminar in Kuwait was a turning point in my life. It signaled new adventures beyond the known. It also served as a reintegration to viewing myself as international citizen of the world, not just as an American. Just like I had felt as an 'international bright young thing' in Japan.

My academy had a free global distribution platform, which was opening a world of opportunity. I was residing in Bend, appreciating it's beauty and regenerative power; living in the town but not of it. It was my home base, but was connected to a much larger picture.

When I flew back to Bend Julie was packed up into countless boxes, which dominated the entryway.

My girl was leaving. It was real.

The vision of her walking our Pomeranian around Drake Park in the morning and kicking the autumn leaves with a latte in her hand had to go. Separate visions had emerged.

Pretty, witty, and strong. I loved that girl. Now she's gone forever. I held myself up as she drove away.

CHAPTER 16

THE BEAUTY
OF YOGA

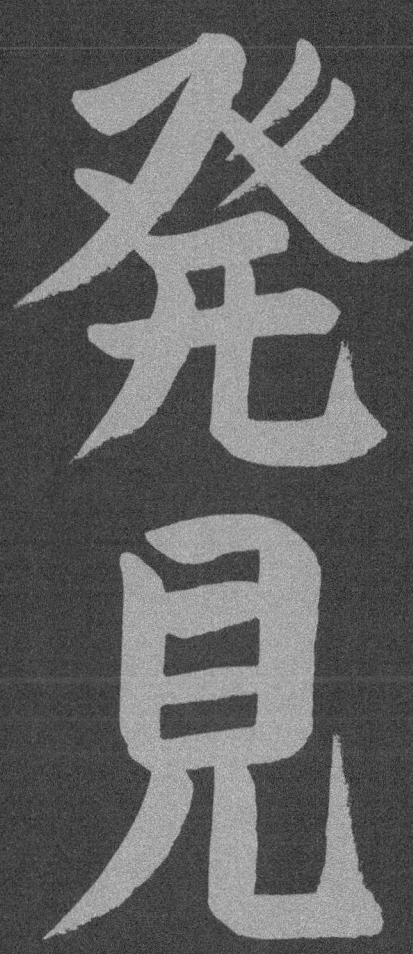

THE BEAUTY OF YOGA

My heart was still wounded from the breakup. I had dated a bit when I first moved to town, but the pool was small.

I met a few nice girls, but nothing that captivated me, until I met Stacey.

She was a sharp girl from the Midwest who discovered yoga in college and instantly knew she wanted to be a professional. She went for it entirely, which I deeply respect.

Stacey was my first teacher, her introductory lessons to Ashtanga were intriguing. The grace with which she placed her hands on the floor and jumped her legs back was so smooth and perfectly cambered that she floated into position.

Her practice was outstanding. Her body was strong and supple, with powerful intent. This was not your average instructor. This was a real yogi, with a real guru, Pattahbi Jois, the founder of Ashtanga.

It's worth noting that Pattahbi Jois and BKS Iyengar, founder of another popular style, both had the same teacher, Tirumalai Krishnamacharya. Two schools. Gracie and Machado. You understand.

She was the most advanced yogi I'd ever seen. Her secret was a daily practice, which had been ongoing for several years.

There are five physical levels of asanas (or postures) in Ashtanga. The first, primary series, is quite difficult. I find it to be a humbling discipline, which, they recommend, takes seven years to complete. That's right, seven years for the first level. Makes two years to blue seem pretty rapid. Perspective.

I moved into a new condo on the Westside of Bend. I was putting a considerable amount of time and energy into yoga to keep my mind right after Julie left. It was a new challenge and there's nothing like throwing yourself into a physical practice to initiate emotional recovery.

I had a definite interest in Stacey, so, one Friday afternoon, just after she led me through my highly modified primary series in the afternoon Ashtanga class, I asked her out to dinner.

She agreed, much to my delight. We dated for a few months. Such great conversations. She had few material possessions, but was well read. Our vibe was harmonious, and we never fought.

As attractive as she was, my respect for her grew from her dedication to her craft, and as a fellow seeker on the path. Strength and beauty combined. She had that warrior spirit. On a different mat.

Purple Belt Requirements

The Blue Belt Requirements DVD had been far more successful than I imagined it would be.

People on and offline were clambering for Purple Belt Requirements. In a lot of ways, I know what people wanted. Same look, same format, same everything, just with more difficult techniques. More advanced techniques. Techniques you would need to know to make it to the level of purple belt.

But I couldn't do that. Purple belt was about synthesizing your own game based on your body type and technical lineage. It was about chaining simple techniques together into combinations, not necessarily doing more complex individual techniques. Complexity naturally arises out of simple and repeated processes.

My idea was this: I present you with a game. A blue print, a framework designed to move you forward in your performance by having a conceptual breakthrough. It's about putting the words you learned at blue belt into sentences at purple. If the techniques don't work for you, then you can substitute them out with others that are more suitable. Dialect is a natural part of language development. This framework allows for variation.

Rick had a custom, cranberry-walled gym on the bottom level of his new house. It was a fitting aesthetic for this disc. Blue belt had me in a blue gi, on green tatami, fading into darkness. Now I was in a black gi, on white mats, with a red wall behind. A different visual motif. Every project had to be different.

We filmed and I edited the footage, putting together positional synopsis clips with a voiceover and an opening monologue, which presented the analogy of learning words at blue belt, and putting them into sentences at purple.

I was trying to do something different with this DVD. Make it more conceptual, rather than "technique" oriented. If you watch it as an early blue, expecting it to be blue belt requirements part two, just wanting more "advanced" techniques, you're probably going to be disappointed.

But if you're ready, if you're ripe for a specific kind of realization, this can be exactly what you're looking for. If you're at the point where you're tired of learning new material, when you're technique'd out, this is your guide to putting together what you know.

You bridge that gap between blue and purple with a personalized skill set. You're setting yourself up to creatively problem solve against other skilled martial artists.

Purple is the mini black belt, allowing you to fully engage and participate in the physical debate. It is a respected rank that indicates an impressive level of physical literacy.

UK Seminar

While the DVDs were being replicated in San Francisco, I took an advanced copy of Purple Belt Requirements on my trip to England.

Rick was also in full media mode, in the process of making a movie about his journey to purple belt. Heading to England with me was going to be one part of the story.

Rick also paid for one of the dojo members to come along and help film the adventure. The cameraman had just got back from his honeymoon, before heading out to the UK with us. After those ten days, I never saw him on the mat again.

I think his wife may have let him have his last hurrah on that adventure. Not a bad way to go out, really.

The full documentary never saw the light of day, but parts of it can be seen on the White Belt Bible. It was the start of a great friendship with Steve and Paul, and I was able to meet a prolific blogger by the name of Can Sonmez.

Seymour Yang "aka Meerkatsu" did a complimentary profile piece for Jiu Jitsu Style magazine on that trip, and a new purple belt named Matt Benyon made it to the seminar, fresh from Japan and putting a lot of energy into his own brand, Scramble. All were fantastic folks passionate about the art.

Can could see where I was going with Purple Belt Requirements. It had the conceptual piece, positional overviews, sparring footage of various belt levels, and even some experimental pieces on the second disc.

"The Spirals of Jiu Jitsu" is the perfect example of this experimental artsy-ness. TJ, Rick and I were just messing around at the dojo when we filmed seven techniques with a high-speed camera TJ had commandeered from work. Using this highly specialized camera capable of shooting three thousand frames per second, we opted for three hundred. It made all the movements look buttery smooth as I floated through the air.

I had just put together a new track, "Can't Talk Now", so I married the brooding music with slow motion techniques, threw in a Musashi quote at the end, and we arrived at something that reminds you that jiu jitsu is an art, not just a game with judges and points in a specific range dictated by a number of rules.

That said, I was offered an opportunity to play that game and showcase my skills at the 2009 World Championships.

I had nothing to lose, and I took the chance.

CHAPTER 17

WORLD CHAMPIONSHIPS

WORLD CHAMPIONSHIPS

Three weeks ago I received a call. An opportunity.

To compete in the world championships.

"Think of doing it as a walk on," urged my sponsor.

And I thought to myself, "Why not?"

After all, my body felt good. No neck, knee, or back issues (largely due to the Ashtanga Yoga practice I'd begun). With regular chiropractic care as the cherry on top for the martial athlete. Everything was aligned for me to have another adventure.

This time, I would do everything differently from my last competition (the 2008 Pan Ams). I made mistakes on several fronts: too many people knew about it, and I felt that I took on the expectations of friends and students. E-mails of encouragement from people I'd never met added to it.

I was stressed, doing everything to cut weight in the last few days, and was grumpy in the process. I felt that I went into the Pan Ams event weakened and sapped. I'd go medium-heavy this year, as opposed to middleweight. I never wanted to cut weight like that again.

Another mistake was spending too much time at the event before the match. Watching a good battle can rob you of energy if you get emotionally swayed through the ups and downs of a roll, especially if you're rooting for a particular player. So this year, I would fly in on Saturday at noon, check into the hotel, and step in there before my division started at 5 p.m. Simply business.

I was also going without ridiculous expectations. All but one person loses at the Worlds. The division I was in is filled with beasts. I would definitely be light for my division, too. Weighing in at home, I was 190 pounds with the gi on. I figured I was giving up 4.5 pounds, but I would later realize I was, in fact, giving up more!

Rick Ellis was the only person I told. He was game to join me, so we hit the road Saturday morning and made the pilgrimage to Southern California: to enter the Walter Pyramid at California State University Long Beach, to represent Harris International.

We got there around 4:30p.m. We watched a few matches and then the middleweight and medium-heavy divisions were called to warm up in the bullpen.

It's a BJJ who's who down on the floor inside the plastic gates. You're shoulder to shoulder with Rickson Gracie, Saulo Ribiero, Victor and Braulio Estima, and many others. Who just bumped my elbow and apologized? Oh, it's Roger Gracie. No problem bro. Please don't collar choke me.

It's tempting to want to shake hands and tell them how much you love their jiu jitsu, what an honor it is to meet them, etc. But it's neither the time nor place, so I kept to myself, warming up lightly and just being positive and relaxed. I kept reminding myself it was just for fun, for the experience, and to have a roll with another black belt. I was happy just to be part of the show and participating in the process.

Preston Rawlings and Louie Cercedez (also a BJJ black belt under Mr. Harris) made a special trip just to provide coaching and said hello to me in the pen. Very thoughtful of them. It really does give the competitor a little extra juice knowing there are souls in the vast Pyramid rooting for them.

My name was called on the loudspeaker and, after a thorough uniform check by IBJJF officials, I weighed in at 182.5 pounds. This positioned me with me 12 pounds to spare in my division, and just 1.5 pounds over the middleweight class.

My first match was against Sebastian Munoz, a representative of Gracie Humaita, Argentina. He bowed onto the mat and I liked him immediately. Respectful. We shook hands and got to work.

Sebastian had a different body type, much thicker and a few inches shorter. I felt out an inside trip, and he responded with a foot sweep of his own, nicking my foot as I stumbled to guard. Two points for him. He immediately passed and received three more.

Not a great start. I escaped and we were back on our feet. I pulled guard aggressively, looking for a flying arm lock. No dice. I shot for a triangle. He shucked it off and I replaced guard. I play my open and half guard for some time. He's dropping his weight on my right leg and knows how to use it. Very strong passing pressure, but he can't quite get around my leg.

It wasn't until about two minutes into the match that I really felt warmed up and flowing. Even though I was down on points, it's never over 'till it's over, and with eight minutes left in the match, I still had time.

About four minutes in, I look at the scoreboard and reaffirm I'm down 0-5. I have to make something happen and, from open guard, I push his head into a sleeve choke. He tries to roll out of it and I follow the change in positions to side mount. My hand is still on his collar and the choke tightens. He taps and it's all over!

It had been a while since I'd had my hand raised in competition. My first win as a black belt, in the World Championships, by submission. Not bad. I was told to return to the bullpen and they would call me for the next match.

I had seen the brackets and knew that, if I got through my first match, Victor Estima would be waiting for me. Victor is the younger brother of Braulio Estima, multiple time BJJ World Champion; being deadly obviously runs in the family. He had won the Pan Ams at brown belt and had just been in the finals of the Professional BJJ Cup held in Abu Dhabi.

I have been a fan of Victor's for some time, after watching him on YouTube, trying to replicate his patented sweep to arm lock from guard. His jiu jitsu is smooth and dynamic. Even my good friend Alicia Anthony, who kept me company in the bullpen for awhile, couldn't help but gush about his game when I told her we were matched.

I thought I'd be back in action within twenty minutes or so, but it ended up being over an hour until I got back onto mat number five. This would be

Victor's first match, and my second of the tournament. We shook hands, fist bumped, and got down to business.

But Victor was much more business than I was, I could tell that right away. Crouched with his hands in front of him, he stared directly into my chest and did not look away. The moment I went to grip, he grabbed me, pulled guard, and immediately went to work on his patented sweep to arm lock technique. I dropped to my knees to avoid the sweep and try to stabilize. He continued to reach for my far knee, undeterred by my attempts at basing and opening his guard.

I knew what he was going for and felt like I was watching it in slow motion. His highlight reel technique was being applied to me. Damn. I felt my left hip touch the ground and knew it was all over. Checkmate, my friend. Checkmate. His leg came over my face and I tapped as my arm extended out. He released with perfect control.

I got owned by Victor Estima and it was a pleasure. I could feel that he's at another level with his competition game. His mental focus, his athleticism, and his game plan of knowing EXACTLY what he's looking for allows him to succeed at the highest levels in this sport.

Of course I was rooting for him to win the entire tournament. Victor arm locked his next opponent and, the following day in the quarter finals, he won a tough and technical match on points against a beastly man in a black gi. I missed his semi final match, which he somehow lost and ended up being awarded the bronze medal. Congratulations Victor!

I felt lucky to have had both matches. I won and lost. Duality at its finest. And there's respect and camaraderie amongst the competitors, too. Sebastian and I have already connected, I'll be sending him a copy of the match, and Victor and I are now Facebook friends. Perhaps we can train together in the future. It would be an honor.

There was a touching and well-produced tribute to Grandmaster Helio Gracie on Sunday before the men's finals. Everyone in attendance was on their feet, clearly reminded upon whose shoulders we stand as we practice this incredible art.

The BJJ of today, when played at the highest level, is strategic, innovative, and often decided by the slimmest of margins. My category was so closely contested in the final match that a referee's decision gave Romulo Barral the victory over Tarsis Humphrey in a ten minute battle without a single point or advantage being scored.

Will I compete again next year? Perhaps. You have to be realistic and realize that to succeed at the World level, you need to have training partners that are also competing and active at that level. The game changes rapidly now that everyone can study matches on YouTube and DVDs, and our martial consciousness continues to expand like no other time in human history.

It's very exciting, and I am thankful to be involved in this process of evolution, at this moment, in this art, and making friends along the way.

CHAPTER 18
AWAKE IN
the DREAM

AWAKE IN THE DREAM

I was driving down the highway from Naples to the Florida Keys to visit my friend Stacey, who had left Bend to take a position teaching at the most beautiful, and well financed, yoga shala I'd ever seen.

There's a feeling of freedom that a car allows, with an open stretch of highway ahead, and a beautiful girl at the destination. Life was exhilarating and endlessly possible. Freedom. Without the dojo. For a few moments.

I could see it all happening as I drove down that highway. One of my students would take over. If I sold it, or gave it away, it didn't matter. I wouldn't have it forever. Maybe it would be Donald. Maybe it would be Neil. I didn't know, but the finish line appeared in my mind on that long stretch of Florida highway.

This trip was a reward to myself for finishing my latest DVD, No Gi Essentials. I had set up a seminar in Naples, Florida, and I was now heading towards the relaxation section of my journey.

At the end of this particular seminar, I offered to roll with everyone. One thing you'll learn as a jiu jitsu professional is that some guys roll cool, some guys roll crazy, and some guys are just plain tough. My instructor once sparred with sixty people in a row in Europe. I probably did a dozen and was thankful I could call it at that.

It can be a risky endeavor. Often the untrained are more dangerous than skilled students, who usually operate within a framework of movements and attacks. You have to be on guard at all times with a wild white belt.

The Academy was in full swing back in Bend. I hired one of my students, Becky, as the dojo manager, and put her in charge of shipping. This lightened my load considerably. DVDs were going out every day. Spreading the word on shiny discs to destinations around the world.

I was doing lots of seminars and received many visitors too. I headed out to Connecticut, Colorado, Calgary, and Virginia for seminars. The UK crew came back again, as well as a cool chap named Dion who visited for two weeks from Australia.

Dion wanted to have an adventure before settling into the nine to five grind of early adulthood, so he trekked to Bend to the dojo he had seen online, and we shared the mat.

We'd cross paths again in England at a seminar while he was living in London. The jiu jitsu world is actually quite small, once you've been in it for a while.

My online presence was paying real dividends, and provided the opportunity for a pilgrims like Dion to connect with a teacher who was on the same path, helping to guide them, even if only for a short leg of the journey.

Of all the instructionals I've produced, No Gi Essentials is probably my favorite. We started shooting and I wanted to do something bold and different with this one.

The production quality was definitely a step up, but the real revolution was the closeness of the camera following the action, producing incredibly candid instruction.

We shared sophisticated technical sequences, but I'm told it was the game theory, rolling narration, and production value that set it apart. In some ways I feel it's my best work. Maybe because, in the back of my mind, I was doing this one for my Dad.

I was haunted by the specter of my father's death. He had been diagnosed with mesothelioma. It's a terrible disease where your lungs harden and you slowly suffocate. Not the worst way to go but still quite grim to think about.

The grief dynamics in my family were tough and emotionally draining. I tried to be a good and dutiful son, seeing my father several times in the last year, but one can always wonder if it's ever enough in that precious final stretch.

I loved my father, but I also felt a certain distance from him. There were two generation gaps between us. We were provided for, and yet I yearned for more. From my father. From my life. In so many ways I wanted to be the opposite of him, but he was an honest, hard working man, and deserving of true respect.

My father grew up in the Great Depression, and began working as a child. He joined the Marines at age seventeen to fight the Japanese in the South Pacific. He never talked about the war, but felt at home at the American Legion and the Veterans of Foreign Wars establishments. That was his dojo. That's where he bonded with the warriors of his generation, and there were very few left by the time he passed.

But in the meantime, I had a business to run, and a vision to achieve. Every aspect of the Academy took energy, but the creativity continued to flow.

I made a custom RDA gi, just for fun, with offset stitching and the kanji for honor embroidered on each shoulder. Jiu Jitsu de Brasil in kanji and kanatana was running down the leg. It looked cool. Another idea brought to life. I loved making it happen.

I was running on all cylinders at this point. No Gi Essentials was a success, while the blue and purple belt DVDs were also selling well. I was flying around the world, making more money than I ever thought I could, and doing something that I loved. That I felt called to do. I imagined that I could do it, and I actually did it.

The most unreal part is that I was so appreciated for doing it. E-mails came from every corner of the globe, and were effusive in their praise. They loved my flow, my technique, the way that I taught. My videos were like no other. I made jiu jitsu beautiful, and they appreciated my efforts as much as I loved the art.

But there's also a trap of attachment that goes along with it. It's easy to get caught up in online praise and measurable celebrity. Is it a drug? For sure. People live and die on that stuff. It's the cocaine of our generation.

Niche fame is a hellava drug, and the Internet has democratized it like never before. I got a taste, I liked it, and I believe I've handled it reasonably well. But not everyone can handle it and stay tethered to reality.

I knew that I was a good jiu jitsu player, but I also recognized the gap between myself and a world-class competitive black belt.

To win a match at the world level is a legitimate indicator of proficiency. To win the entire tournament is not just another level of performance, it's several levels of performance beyond where I was at in my dedication to the craft. I knew it. I could feel it. It's a reality check that most people will never get in their lives.

I was not near that level, nor was I willing to do everything you have to do to be a consistent contender. There's a lot to it. High level is still not at THAT level. I knew my place. I always have. It's important to learn to be comfortable there.

People tell me I'm a good teacher, and it's the synergy of those skills that people enjoy. You don't have to be the best in the world to share the art and make a very real contribution. But you should be the best student and teacher that you can be.

The creative energy was at work like no other time before. My life was full of purpose, and there was a swagger and confidence to my actions, much different than in my twenties.

The dojo was getting more colorful. I promoted James Malone and Rick Ellis to purple belt. There were lots of blue belt demonstrations as well. I promoted my first female blue belt, which was a proud moment. Good energy, all the way around.

We had been hitting the SubLeague submission-only tournaments for some time, and doing well. Particularly the women. Donald was my first gold medalist as a male. These are small milestones on the teacher's path. The gold medals were an indicator that my lessons, and training methods, were effective.

Watching your students win is one of the most rewarding moments you can have as a jiu jitsu instructor. To see them do what they do best, playing their game on the mat, expressing themselves fully, regardless of the outcome, is a priceless experience.

Submission only suited our academy style better than the points game. It encouraged aggression and opportunity. I never taught for points. To me, jiu jitsu should aim for submission, towards finishing the fight.

I was bummed to find out that Rick was moving to Hawaii, but there was a definite silver lining. He asked me to move in to his killer pad until a buyer was found. I agreed without hesitation. It was a dope house, with drop away views, bold colors and a custom gym on the bottom floor.

The king's palace had been opened to the prince, and I was deeply appreciative. I was living large as a jiu jitsu instructor and was fully awake in the dream. My father, meanwhile, crept closer and closer to passing from one realm to the next.

CHAPTER 19

Taking the Medicine

AIFU

BELOVED FATHER

TAKING THE MEDICINE

I'm a seeker. I'm explorer. A timid psychic cosmonaut.

You can sometimes get a glimpse of that next realm, or at least something outside of this one. That shift in perspective can reframe everything.

With that intention of reframing my life, I quietly approached The Medicine, Ayahuasca.

I had been invited to go with my acupuncturist to an upcoming ayahuasca ceremony. He had been apprenticing under a Shaman in Peru, and was assisting another shaman in an upcoming ceremony.

Ayahuasca is a powerful hallucinogenic brew used as a spiritual sacrament. It is often administered in an extended ceremony beginning at sundown, and ending in the early morning hours.

I did it with the intent of honoring my father, and understanding a little more about this transition from one world to the next. The setting was plush, a friends house, with a small group of aspirants gathered together.

I drank the medicine that the shaman poured for me, as I knelt before him.

It tasted strange. Alien. Alkaloid. I sat upright as I waited for it to take effect. Which it did. Quite strongly.

Forty five minutes after ingestion, I felt the molecules unfolding inside of me, swaying my body to a new and slower rhythm, working it's way through me. It had taken control.

It was a bumpy ride. I purged a lot. Out of my mouth, but spiritually as well. Attachments of all kinds were released. It was a psychosomatic cleansing.

Visions of the guru I almost sat with also came to mind. His face flashed in front of me, followed by dark occult symbols, as the rollercoaster dove down. My stomach dropped out as I found myself shooting through an alternate universe, and riding the snake all the way to Valhalla.

My friend reassured me "Don't worry, Sensei. We'll pull that stuff out of you."

Maybe I hadn't fully escaped the clutches of the guru. Perhaps just going to his community was enough to get his hooks in, and the shamans were pulling out the hooked legs and long bodies of dark spiritual centipedes.

Perspective radically shifts in those states. You begin to see how the world works through the lens of spiritual warfare. You're allowed a glimpse to a higher order to the dynamics of creation.

The vomiting was high volume, in terms of decibels. An eleven on the amp. At one point, I was purging so loudly that my friend had to intervene.

"Could you keep it down? You're kinda… starting to freak the other people out."

Even in my stupor, I apologized to everyone. Not a party drug my friends. Nor for the feint of heart. But suffering begets wisdom, and I was looking for a deeper understanding.

You need a navigator, a shaman, to trust in, to lean on, and guide you through this multi hour journey of hallucinations and otherworldly experience.

After it was all over, there was a swing in my step the next day, as I found myself unconsciously bouncing my foot to a song on the radio. I was happy to have just survived the experience, and felt fortunate to have been able to drink it in a beautiful home, with a few trusted friends, rather than having to fly to Amazonia to feel it for myself. I came out stronger and healthier for the experience.

I was also willing to take a sacrament in my own realm, on my own mat, in a crucible of my own design.

I wanted to test for my second-degree black belt under Mr. Harris. It had been four years since getting my black and, to be perfectly honest, I felt like I deserved it.

I had given a lot to the jiu jitsu community, doing extensive work online, showcasing the art through demonstrations and instructional videos. I competed at the World Championships. My students were winning at tournaments, my personal game had come a long way, and my teaching game was getting polished. I was a full professional.

Still dipping heavily into Ashtanga, I was looking mean and lean. Not lifting much, despite having the weight room in the basement. I should have been though. I should have been more serious about my conditioning. My second-degree black belt exam was coming up, and I knew I was going to suffer. How much, and the manner in which that suffering was dispensed was still up in the air.

Mr. Harris didn't have a list of requirements for the level, and I had no idea what to expect. At a seminar in Calgary, he told fellow black belt Brian Bird and I to focus on collar chokes, but that was just a single point of focus, which didn't really warn me for the physical challenge that lay ahead.

The schedule that Saturday was a two hour seminar, my demonstration, a lunch break, then another two hour session. I was assisting Mr. Harris that morning, correcting technique, chatting it up, and generally in good spirits, excited about the day and the upcoming challenge.

But I should have been warming up. Mr. Harris may have actually been hinting for me to warm up, as he kept showing me kettle bell exercises in between techniques. I did a few swings and set it down. I should have kept going. I should have been sweating profusely because I was about to go straight into sparring, as cold as a man can be.

It began with Jeff, a training partner from my Seibukan Jujutsu days. Largest guy in the room, with a very good mount position. Mr. Harris had seen this the day before, during his blue belt test, when he dominated his opponents from the top.

I had to escape Jeff's mount twice, then Chris, a spry fifty-something,

Shotokan black belt and BJJ blue, held me from side control. I escaped twice, and then repeated that pattern with various partners, and various positions, as Mr. Harris saw fit.

He granted me a few breaks, where I stepped outside and he captivated students with stories of the old days, about the first generation of BJJ in the United States.

There was never a thought of quitting, but it was not going as smoothly as I had hoped. I checked my pulse once I got outside and it was racing. Over 180 BPM. After sucking in as much fresh air as possible, and feeling some pressure to return to the mat, I checked my pulse again.

WTF? It was basically the same. My heartbeat wasn't going down at all. Frightening. Should have done more metabolic conditioning this entire time. Another round was coming. The ride wasn't over yet.

I had been dishing out a lot of medicine with these online demonstrations, pushing the students to show their heart in the final round. Now it was time for me to take my dose and it was a little rougher than I anticipated.

James, one of my purple belts, gave me a lot of encouragement during the entire test, and I rolled with him more than once. During the second roll, I reached a fatigue threshold where the tabled turned and I was on the defensive. That was the signal for Mr. Harris to step in to check if I still had the heart of a black belt.

When a man like Mr. Harris pins you, it is a feeling like no other. He attacks your breath with his body, incapacitating you at the most fundamental level. Your brain is telling you that it's not even possible for you to move. Yet you must. You have to keep going.

My master allowed me to submit him with a cross choke from mount, after considerable struggle on my end.

I received my second degree, but it was a rougher reentry than I expected.

I continued to pay my dues.

Natural Separations

"Leave your ego at the door" is a popular saying in BJJ circles.

What they don't tell you is that you have to lose that ego many times in the journey. Once, as a white belt, of course. But again at every rank along the way. Even at black.

The BJJ journey is a lengthy endeavor. Paths diverge on such a long road. Teachers and students separate. It's a natural occurrence. The most important thing to consider is how to play the long-term game, both as a student, and as an instructor.

You may think, as I did, that if you're a gifted instructor, you'll retain almost all of your students. Those that come into contact with you, and adhere to your tutelage, will remain loyal and dedicated. After all, you're a charismatic teacher, with real physical skill to back it up.

Now here's the truth: you will lose every student that comes to you. Eventually. Over time. How gracefully can you let go of things? You have to learn to celebrate the release. But it's easier said than done.

Martial arts are difficult. Brazilian Jiu Jitsu is particularly hard. People will drop out. They will quit. Or, as Chris Hauter puts it in the documentary "Roll: Jiu Jitsu in SoCal":

"It's not who's good. It's who's left."

You saw it happen as a student, so don't be surprised or take it personally as an instructor. It doesn't mean your product isn't good, that your skills aren't genuine, that your teaching isn't addictive. Jiu jitsu is an art that requires a lot of energy, and not everybody has that time or attention.

It's them, not you. Let them go. Wish them well. Do not take it personally.

This is advice I wish I could have given myself.

As a blue belt and certified instructor under Mr. Harris, Jimmy was teaching a few guys before I took his suggestion and moved to Bend.

I brought him to blue belt in San Diego, promoted him to purple in Bend, and eventually led him to his brown. That's when Jimmy approached me about leading a grappling class at a local Crossfit gym, to realize his vision of taking really good athletes, and teaching them advanced jiu jitsu right away.

I wasn't hot on the idea, and recommended training with the crew at RDA instead. Jimmy had been doing his own thing for a while, and he wasn't spending that much time at the academy anymore. I honestly felt he could go farther by training more closely with me. Even though Jimmy was an excellent athlete, and supremely coordinated, he could still find challenge with many of my larger, and well controlled players. I felt it was the best path for his development.

Jimmy opened up shop anyway. I tried to work with it for about a year, when it was just a private club in a commercial space. But once he began charging tuition, I felt that he needed to be an affiliate, just like the other affiliates around the world.

If he was going to be my student, accept rank, use my lineage and teach for profit, he was going to have to accept the other half of the deal.

Jimmy was my friend, and I wanted it to work. Others saw it as a straight up dis, and an inevitable separation. I went to great lengths to establish a special training environment that benefitted him greatly, and I simply asked for him to honor a standard professional courtesy.

I gave him a few options for moving forward. First was simply paying the affiliation fee and keeping his facility open, with full support and integration with the main school.

Second was closing his facility and coming back to teach at the Academy.

Third was being independent and doing his own thing entirely.

We talked about it and, after several days, he came back to me with his decision. True to form, he wanted to keep his facility open, but not pay the entire fee. He let me know that the school was generating more than enough revenue to cover it, but he wanted his own deal.

So I gave him what he wanted. His own deal. Option Three.

It hurt to release my top student, but he always wanted to be on his own, to forge his own path. Now he really could.

I needed some time away, so I flew to Alaska to recharge, visit my father for the last time, and reassess the direction I was heading in. Letting Jimmy go was tough for me emotionally. Devastating, really.

Was this the price of being a professional? I was starting to see that being a teacher is not just about leading people, it's also about letting them go. Even those that have been with you for some time. Even those who were there at the start of your life, and now you're seeing them at the end of theirs.

That December, I flew to Alaska to attend my father's funeral. It was a bleak military burial. Ritual is embedded in all of our lives, of course. From your church to the mat to the opening of your favorite show. But to be lead by these soldiers, so precise and well versed in their duties, was profound.

These Marines led the burial for my family. These Marines led people in their darkest hour. Again and again. In all situations. Rain, shine, or in cold December air surrounded by snow.

The day had never been so empty. The light was present but hollow. Or maybe that's just how I felt.

The Marines who folded the flag did not know my father, but they channeled a gravitas for all the fallen, past and present, including the man that lead me to this moment.

When the flag was placed in my mother's hands, I had no words. Only appreciation for these men and that ritual, which was performed to ease my pain, to dissipate this grief.

If true budo is to protect all life, then these soldiers guard the exit of that life, ensuring safe passage for one special man.

Semper Fi, father. Semper Fi.

CHAPTER 20
THINGS FALLING APART

謙虚

THINGS FALLING APART

Bigger and better.

Onwards and upwards.

Boom or Bust.

This is the American business model.

This is the American way.

Most martial arts instructors work very very hard. Lots of classes, all day long, with a big kids program as the bread and butter. Over time, you get an education in the martial arts school system. Phone scripts, parent nights and black belt programs.

I could never really get into it. Was I a professional martial arts instructor? Or a new media entrepreneur?

My lease was up at the Third Street dojo and I moved the Academy to a bigger, better, more modern space. Of course, this created a much larger overhead, and it took a considerable investment to get it all dialed in. I purchased new mats, new construction, new paint and new artwork.

I was required to hire an engineer, twice, to mathematically prove that the non-load bearing walls we put in for the office and dressing rooms wouldn't fall over if pushed. That was just one of the city stipulations that was ridiculous, and in many ways, simply a money grab. The city could take a look at your plans in a month, or they could do it that night. For the right price.

At one point, after complying with several regulations, the plans were once again rejected. Why? They didn't feel the two large, ADA approved bathrooms were going to be enough. They wanted me to put in two more, in a three thousand, six hundred square foot space. Four bathrooms? It made no sense at all.

I called my new landlord to let him know that I couldn't move forward. I couldn't afford to do what they were asking. Once he made a frantic call to the head of the city's building department, things were smoothed over and my plans were approved. Just like that.

The entire process was obstructionist and it made me look at regulation and government very differently. I suddenly understood why people might want to succeed from a union.

Other people would have built without permits, but again, that's not how I roll. The subtle paranoia that comes with doing deals under the table is not something I'm comfortable with. It simply isn't worth it to me. But regulatory frustrations weren't fun either.

Business models change, as well as markets. When I was launching the Academy, the most important thing was to get people on the mat and create a sense of community and camaraderie.

In that spirit, I let one of my best guys train for free. He was positive, intelligent, honest, hardworking, and good on the mats.

Fast forward four and a half years and our friend was having BJJ adventures in other states and even other countries. But he still wasn't supporting his home academy, and something felt off about that.

I'm a generous man, but everyone has their limits. My policy of letting instructors train for free was working for him, but it wasn't working for us, and it didn't feel sustainable. You don't want to resent your students, but if one person gives, and the other one takes, that can be the result. Relationships like that only lasts so long. So I made a change in policy as we moved into the new space.

The new rule was that no one trained for free, but tuition for instructors was heavily discounted. That seems fair. I wanted everyone contributing, everyone with some skin in the game. The dollar amount wasn't that important. It was the principle that mattered most.

That's when life threw me a curve ball. Everyone, including the instructor which initiated the change, was completely on board with the policy shift, as Becky reached out to handle the process. Being banker and sensei is never comfortable, so my assistant was the perfect intermediary as we transitioned to a new policy in a new environment.

Then James, my right hand man at the Academy, told me he couldn't go along with it, and sent me a letter of resignation via email.

I followed up immediately, telling him to stop talking crazy. He couldn't be serious. Resign from the academy? Things were just about to get AMAZING at the new space. With my new college class? Why would he want to leave now?

I don't know. Perhaps he stopped seeing me as his teacher, and saw me as more of a friend, because we had hung out socially. The lines had been blurred.

Some are adept at separating roles within the same individual. They can be a friend, student, teacher, colleague or whatever. But not everyone's like that.

The ego flares at purple belt. I've seen it happen. It happened for me. Not everyone retains that student or white belt mentality. The temptations of the ego are always unfolding. It's hard to balance a white belt mentality with the pursuit of an alpha male status. But it can be done.

A purple belt has already become someone else: a submission artist, capable of applying powerful techniques, and often teaching or helping in classes. They are something more than they were before. They may see themselves differently.

Please don't fall for that ego trip. I'm telling you now so that you know in advance and can cautiously guard against it.

I wasn't the only mentor James was initiating a split with. It appeared, from the outside, to be a psycho spiritual crisis, where he wanted complete separation from several key players in his life.

He framed it as a money issue, but that was just the polite way of saying he didn't want to bow anymore. Some people bow to no man, and ask no man to bow to them. I understand that mentality as well. But James didn't want to bow, yet he wanted others to bow to him. I couldn't support that.

Others saw it more simply. He had to be the man, and couldn't accept a circumstance in which he wasn't.

I tried to work it out with him, even taking a long final meeting, but he had to go his own way. I lost a student and a friend. So we shook hands and he forged his own path. He sent me a modest letter appreciating the role he played in the Academy, and I thanked him for his efforts as well.

Hypergamy

Before we went our separate ways, James introduced me to a girl named Sophia. Months later, and long forgotten, she reached out to me via Facebook on Valentine's Day as I was coming back from a vacation in Palm Springs.

I was single at the time, so we met for a drink and hit it off.

Sophia was a stunner. The kind of girl who turns the heads of every man she's around.

She looked a little bit like Morgan Fairchild. I actually recorded Morgan back in San Diego. She was the only client I felt a little star struck by. She was very sexy and still had it. Voluptuous, and tastefully blinged-out. She had that LA look but was down to earth. Does it get any better than that?

Mrs. Fairchild had to drop in a few lines for a new pilot she was in. The session went smoothly, and the conversations were cordial. I had never been smitten behind the booth. This was a new thing.

The production coordinator took a look at me after the session and totally called me out.

"Roy has a cru-ush!"

Of course I did. The divine feminine had just graced me for an hour.

So it was with Sophia. Another representative of the divine feminine. Since I was already living like a king, a girl like her fit the part. It made sense for the popular BJJ instructor to be with the hottest girl in the room.

She was more than hot, though. She was intelligent. Poised. A wonderful writer. Thoughtful as well.

Beauty is a powerful beast. It can distract you when you need your discernment the most. It can make you re-categorize red flags into stunning shades of orange. It can keep you up at night. It can make you go back on the things you believe.

Early on with Sophia, there were some jealousy issues that I found deeply unsettling, so I asked her about it. Why was she so jealous? I loved her and she had nothing to worry about, or accuse me of. Of course opportunities existed, but I was content with being with her.

She told me she had been diagnosed with condition that would help explain her behaviors: Borderline Personality Disorder (BPD). She urged me to look it up and get educated. I didn't. I skipped that part.

So what if she's a little moody, I thought. How bad could that be?

I was naive, and she gave me fair warning. I was enchanted by her looks, and distracted by the dojo. The academy presented it's own comedic episodes and dramas, replete with all the dynamics of a clan of fighters.

There was also a shifting media landscape, in which my attention had now turned to apps and app development rather than DVD's. There was a lot to juggle personally and professionally, at home, and abroad.

Six months into dating Sophia, I booked a trip to Monterey, with a few of those days spent at the secluded mountain retreat Tassajara.

She was expecting a proposal, but something felt off. I wanted to propose, but not yet. We had only been through good times together. I didn't feel like I truly knew her.

When we returned to Bend, it was never the same. We broke up and got back together, tethered by a frayed emotional cord.

I flew to Mississippi for a seminar with my friend and student Alan Shade. In a terrible omen, my knee popped twice as someone spun under me for a deep half guard. I had torn my ACL badly. I didn't know to what extent it was damaged, but I knew it was the worst knee injury of my life, and I still had to do a three hour seminar the next morning.

Those are the moment you earn your man card all over again. I taught a seminar on wrist locks and standing jiu jitsu which was well received. That's when you know you're a professional. When you can improvise and deliver even when you're not at full capacity, or even close to capacity. You can keep going, even when things are falling apart.

I came back to Bend, broken. The next weekend Sophia saw an old friend, a talented musician, who was doing a concert in Portland. They connected. He promised everything I couldn't give her. She could pick a house and he would buy it. She could raise his children, her son, and the little girl she wanted to bring into the world so badly. It was straight hypergamy.

She carved my heart out as she sat on my couch and told me about this deal she'd made. How she loved him, and how he loved her.

I told her it was a fantasy, that she couldn't be the only one who had heard this before, that he was still with someone else. She was resolute. She had opened her heart to him.

The truth is, I wasn't ready to step up like this guy was. I wasn't ready for her son or a new baby.

But my ego, in case you missed out that I had one, was destroyed. Outbid by a white rapper. That shit was whack.

There was a dark night of the soul where I couldn't sleep at all. What was happening here? I was a black belt in Brazilian Jiu Jitsu. But that didn't mean anything. Nothing I could do on the mat could get her back. I felt powerless.

BECOMING THE BLACK BELT

I had a beautiful house, a beautiful car, and a beautiful dojo, and all of it all of it meant nothing if I couldn't have her. What good were these things if they weren't protecting her and her son?

My soul felt damaged, and I was not the same for a while. If there was ever a karmic payday for the broken hearts in my life, this was it. Repaid in full.

It hurt that she loved him. As far as loving me, she said she felt nothing.

"In my mind, I know that I love you. But in my heart, in here," she said, as she touched her chest, "there's nothing. It's just dead."

I wasn't delivering on the goods, and Sophia wanted more.

My buddy Brendan had been there before, in a relationship with similar dynamics, and he helped me understand where she was coming from. He gave me an article from Psychology Today that I should have looked up long ago. Some of the behaviors I read on those pages I had seen played out in real life, word for word.

She wasn't the right fit. I missed so many signs, yet she had given me adequate warning. All is fair in love and war, I suppose.

Winter had come. My knee was broken. I was depressed, but my heart was still beating. Down but not out.

I just needed a place to recover for a while. I needed a place to heal.

CHAPTER 21
A SECOND GOLDEN ERA

JITSUGEN

夢実現

REALIZE YOUR DREAMS

A SECOND GOLDEN ERA

A good friend had a condo in Hawaii that he rarely used, so I camped there for a month to heal my heart, and my nose, which had just been through surgery to help me breathe a little better.

Overlooking that ocean, my problems seemed very small.

It was a contemplative month, and I accepted an invitation to visit the island of Mauritius for a seminar. It was also an opportunity to meet up with my friend Stacey. She flew over from India, after doing her advanced yoga training in Mysore, the birthplace of Ashtanga, on route to Malibu.

Mauritius is considered the Hawaii of Africa, and it's richest nation. Originally colonized by the French, it sits to the right of Madagascar and next to the island of Reunion.

My seminar host and his lovely wife set us up at a beachside resort, and the entire week was a success. Before this leg of the journey, I saw my friend Ahmed in Kuwait, and did a series of seminars at his Gracie Barra school.

The Middle East. Africa. That kind of itinerary earned me extra screenings at customs. But once you've been on the road like that, there's an inertia to keep going. It had never been more clear that I could go anywhere in the world and share my skills.

I wanted to see more of the world. Asia was a real possibility. I had been there as a teenager. Perhaps I was meant to live abroad as an expat. Bend was chosen with purpose because it allowed me to focus on media development but, after six years, the town was feeling a little small.

I had also, finally, reached a point where the revenue streams I established through my media projects were sufficient to step away from the dojo. I didn't have to teach anymore. But I had already made several commitments and, as a professional, it was important to see them through.

I explored legal options for getting out of my lease. Lease laws are ironclad in Oregon and my landlord was not open to a parting of ways. I had the travel itch, but I also had a strong dojo and a clientele I felt a responsibility towards. It wasn't quite time, but my long term art project was heading towards the finish line.

I doubled down. Even though I had suffered a period of professional burnout and personal stress, I was going to make this academy better than ever.

A few of members began grumbling that it wasn't like it used to be. It wasn't quite as fun. It wasn't, for a while. Seasons change. Fields lay fallow.

I listened to my students, then completely quashed that negativity. I directed them to focus on the positive. Yes, many people from earlier generations were gone, but quite a few were still on the mats, and we had plenty of folks signing up and flying in from around the world to train. Just because it's different doesn't mean it can't be amazing. Appreciate this moment, because this moment is someone else's golden era.

Day classes were where the action was. People made it a priority to be there. It often required planning and even packing up the night before. Nights were reserved for beginner classes and for an accredited no gi class, run through the local college.

That class, which I lobbied the academic institution for years to get, exposed me to a really surprising cross section of people. People that would never have ordinarily stepped foot into a martial arts academy. People that had done little to no exercise in their lives. Yet they discovered they could do jiu jitsu. They discovered a little bit more about who they were, and who they were capable of becoming.

I was still the responsible adult in the room, though, and an employer. My first secretary, Becky, was a godsend, and eventually went on to nursing school. My second assistant, an artsy rock climber who really didn't even like jiu jitsu, wasn't the perfect fit, but we parted on good terms when I released her. The third had a knack for social media and love of photography.

All of my assistants were strong, hardworking and intelligent women, and all of them contributed significantly to the development of the academy. Though underrepresented in jiu jitsu by sheer numbers, women can be powerful ambassadors of the art.

Employee relationships can get complicated, however. One of my assistants accused a respected physician in the academy of groping her on the mat. I was traveling at the time. The scenario didn't make sense, but since I believe in backing my employees, I felt compelled to have a conversation with the client.

It's not impossible that a successful man with a stunning wife would indulge in inappropriate behavior, but it was hard to understand his motivation to do so. On any level.

I had a private meeting with the doctor. We talked. I found the accusation by my assistant to be groundless, and noted that a little hysteria might be at hand.

That was one of several incidents that had me reach out to an HR specialist to create an employee handbook. Another sign that the machine was growing.

Was the institution of the business getting more energy than the message I wanted to share? How much was I sharing and explaining the art vs. running the business day to day? How much was I growing as an individual? As a martial artist?

Part of me longed for a simpler situation.

The good news was my students continued to advance in mat skills and general bad-assery. Two of the leaders in the Academy were prepping hard to represent at the Gracie Worlds. That was one of the competitions I wanted to be there for.

Byron came to me as an experienced martial artist, but gladly donned a white belt. He propelled himself up the ranks to purple and, as a strong competitor, I knew that he would have an excellent shot at winning the title.

Donald wanted to compete at brown belt, and had been seriously dieting to make weight, even riding down on the plane with me in a silver sweat suit. Airline security loved that. After weigh-ins, we broke his fast with a sushi dinner and prepared for war the next day.

Simply put, they killed it. Two competitors, two gold medals, two Gracie World Champs. Gracie Worlds isn't the largest tournament, but its submission only format is not for the meek. Somebody is going to tap when you step on that mat. That suited our style.

If no one is submitted in the earlier rounds by the allotted time limit, then neither competitor advances. There are no time limitations in the finals. Guys reach deep, often several times, to finish matches. You get the chance to prove how much you want it.

I was so proud of my guys. Both were special athletes and competitors, both had been loyal and dedicated students. The two go hand in hand.

A Glimpse of the Future

Robert Zeps, BJJ philanthropist and black belt under Nelson Monteiro, reached out to me with regard to being a judge at a new event called Metamoris, and expressed a few kind words about my aikido as well. He studied directly under the great Kazuo Chiba, someone I admired as an Aikido practitioner.

Chiba was one of the original students of Morihei Ueshiba, founder of Aikido. His Aikido worked. There are stories of him going down to the docks in Tokyo to pick fights and test those skills, even offering his opponents a knife to make it more interesting. He was also an advocate of cross training in judo and boxing for a complete skill set. He knew the truth of combat, and as a "hard style" Aikido master, he was revered through the spectrum of aikido schools around the world.

Ralek Gracie and I then began a lengthy correspondence, but he eventually went in a more seasoned direction with the judges, and simply set me up with some nice tickets. TJ drove up from his deployment in San Diego and we enjoyed a stellar show of top tier martial artists.

I felt it was a huge step forward, and a glimpse of the future. Submission fighting should be just as viable as an athletic endeavor as baseball, basketball, and soccer. People just need the right kind of exposure, the right presentation. Metamoris had that quality of broadcast, and the level of presentation, that the art deserved.

I was gearing up for a new kind of adventure as well: Russia. I had a prospective affiliate in a talented purple belt, named Igor. My assistant had been speaking to him for months now, and I knew jiu jitsu was exploding throughout Eastern Europe. He was looking for guidance, not just technically, but in terms of presentation, entrepreneurship and vision. Once we met, it was a natural fit.

The Middle East, Africa, and now Russia. Igor treated me well, and I also met a captivating young woman named Katerina. She was a friend and member of Igor's online business groups. After spending an afternoon together in Moscow, I felt like I had to see her again.

We kept in touch on Facebook, and she made a few trips to the USA. Russian and Eastern European women can be so stunning. It wasn't meant to be, but I appreciated every moment of our East-West connection.

Things continued to steam forward. We hosted a Brandon Mullins seminar, which was fantastic. Smart, technical, and a true student of the game. Definitely an OG for the American BJJ scene.

I sought to bring the best of the best to my students with the guest instructors I introduced. Obviously, Mr. Harris had been blowing the minds of my students for many years.

Marcos "Yemaso" Torregrossa delivered a very cool seminar, loaded with cutting edge competition techniques, then he flew to Brazil to capture the gold medal at the Master's World Championships. It was a strong statement that the seminar content was good.

A personal highlight was having brothers David and Daniel Camarillo each share their skills in the space. They are young masters, and their movements are artistic.

This academy, as a whole, was a dream come true. What an honor to be able to share that dream with others, especially those you respect and admire.

Real Life Applications

Donald, accountant by day, had become head of security at a popular nightclub in town. It was the kind of place you hit at the end of a wet and wild evening.

If you found yourself in the mood, you could definitely find a fight. Monkey dancing could be accommodated on all levels. Stabbings happened, but mainly it was fisticuffs. Donald kept the peace and, over the years, many of the Academy students were temporary security there. Even Becky choked out a girl on a particularly wild night.

Donald used his jiu jitsu many times in those situations. Judo on the dance floor, as well as rear naked chokes, wrist locks, pins, and even kimuras were applied from time to time. D did get sucker punched badly once but, considering the number of altercations he was able to quell peacefully, his success rate was impressive.

We all get sucker punched now and then. The key is to not overreact. Donald kept it cool.

In contrast, I briefly had a student who worked security at another place in town. He was rumored to be aggressive in policing and often taunted patrons. One day he picked a fight with the wrong guy, a bodybuilder, who tackled him through a plate glass window. Either one could have died. It was a dangerous situation for both spectators and combatants.

The bandaged bouncer came to the dojo and told me his side of the story. He described his girlfriend's reaction when she walked into the hospital room.

"The pain in her eyes was too much," he said. He knew he had to quit that job then and there.

"I just couldn't do that to her again."

Meanwhile, the story from his employer is that he was fired.

So who are you going to believe? Personally, I tend to believe the employer. You can't have somebody representing your business who creates problems, rather than solving them, or risks the security of your clientele to satisfy an urge. It's not professional.

Separations can be tough, but you make them happen for the good of the organization.

This is what a leader does. It's not always easy, and often misunderstood.

There's a wonderful story of the Zen master Hakuin. Late in life, he was accused of fathering a child with a local girl. The angry parents confronted him and gave him the child to care for. "Is that so?" was his only response, and immediately went about protecting and raising this precious new life.

Years later, the girl confessed it wasn't that Zen master at all, it was actually the son of a man from the fish market. She had lied. When the parents revisited Hakuin and confessed this revelation, he simply replied "Is that so?" and gave the child back without any hesitation.

A model of non-attachment for us all.

CHAPTER 22
THIRD DEGREE BLACK

THIRD DEGREE BLACK

One peaceful morning, coming home from a particularly good Ashtanga session, my body felt good. My mind was calm. I was aligned. Loose. I thought to myself.

"Wouldn't it be nice to do more yoga and less jiu jitsu, and feel this way all the time?"

That thought actually struck fear into me, because jiu jitsu is what I did. That was my profession. It was how I was known, and it opened doors I never could have imagined. In this niche world, I had respect on a national and international level. That's definitely something for the ego to hold onto. I had invested so heavily in this that there was a fear of loss if I didn't have the dojo, even though that's what I secretly yearned for.

I was tired. Tired of the business, and a little burnt out on the art. There was a sameness to it all. Once you invest fully in a technology, you can begin to see its limitations.

I knew what I wanted to do. I had known for a long time, but was just too afraid to admit it.

I wanted out. The dojo, this place of exploration, had become a cell. Not for the students. Just for me. I felt trapped.

Eight years is a long time to be leading people up the mountain. You may not believe it, but you can get injured simply helping others and, in fact, you should expect it. Yet you still have to come through for them. It's not easy being the man.

This art demands a lot from you. Physically. Technically. Emotionally. Economically. The demands of jiu jitsu temper your spirit in a deeply beneficial way, but it can also drain you. Overtraining happens. Having to be there, having to teach, having to represent, all the time. There is a price of admission, and I paid it more than once.

The injuries had begun to accumulate. I had ACL tears on both knees and, on Katerina's second visit, I tore the ligaments in my left elbow badly. I fell into a lazy kimura at a weak angle. It was just something I tried. An experiment that backfired big time.

My student pulled his fist up and reversed the Kimura so fast I couldn't let go. I heard the tendon tear like a gi ripping in two. I kept going, and I didn't want to admit the extent of the damage for several days. Pain and denial.

To add insult to injury, I had just signed a contract with Go Pro to provide them with ten gigs of jiu jitsu footage, after they watched my video "The Tipping Point."

They wanted it right away, to intersperse with the winter sports of the Sochi Olympics, but I was out of commission for at least four months with this injury.

I had also planned to do a new DVD of extended narration over some sparring, called "Pure Rolling" but that had to be shelved as well. This injury ground everything to a halt.

I could see a larger picture in front of me. Running a martial arts academy had been fun and rewarding, but BJJ felt like a limited world. I secretly yearned to be part of a larger conversation.

The Last Seminar

I scheduled Mr. Harris to come up in October for his annual seminar, and also asked to do my third degree black belt examination during that time.

I was going to be well prepared. Warmed up and ready to go. I didn't want to have to live through another "shock to my system" experience like my second degree. Elevating the heart rate that quickly, through a cold system, was rather hellish when you can't quit.

I suffered for that one. Not as badly as my first degree, but there was a touch of moaning involved.

Most BJJ instructors don't test for degrees on their black belt. It's more of a time in service thing. One stripe every three years.

But I wanted to make it real, make it official. To take the medicine one last time. I knew it would be the last time, and the last seminar.

I drove up to Portland every week for a series of private lessons with Andy Hung, and crashed with my friend Jenny whom I'd known for almost twenty years. It was a great ritual: a meditative drive, culinary delights and top notch instruction from a true judoka.

Andy tuned up my tachi waza, which is exactly what Mr. Harris was looking for. I called him on one of those long drives, checked in about the seminar, and what he expected technically. He specifically wanted my uchimata and tai otoshi brushed up on. Then we moved on to heavier things.

"Mr. Harris. I don't know if I want to do it anymore. I don't think I can do it another three to five years. I'm feeling burnt out."

He had been there. Of course he had been there. Mr. Harris knew the answers because he had paid the price for the knowledge. On the mat, in the teaching game and in disseminating knowledge to people around the world.

He recommended getting out. He told me that he had the Harris Academy for seventeen years, but ending it at fifteen would have been perfect. He knew the feeling I was describing, and gave the kind of advice that had been hard earned through personal experience.

Every martial arts school starts out as a brotherhood, and ends as a business. The first four and a half years were a pleasure, a brotherhood of blood sweat and tears.

The last three and a half were more business, with more boundaries, and more enforcement.

Even if the vibe was less fraternal, it was still fantastic. So many classes, seminars, and rites of passage were generated there, borne there and, luckily, captured on film. Take a look and you'll get a feeling for what it was like. It was a very special place.

To me, it's always been more about those moments than tournament victories. I know distinguished lineages who primarily see jiu jitsu as a competitive endeavor. They celebrate the art through matches and gold medals. Others see it through a lens of self-defense, or with a free fight component, whether that's true vale tudo, or modern MMA competitions.

I teach the middle path, the kind of jiu jitsu that can shift easily to any realm. Once you understand how to intuitively move and generate leverage through your body, you can study many styles or dialects and appreciate their nuance, bio mechanical principles, strategy and techniques.

I needed to wrap up a lot during that last seminar. I promoted a few blues, several purples, and awarded TJ his overdue brown. Just when everyone thought the promotions were over, I clapped my hands and placed a single black belt in the center of the mat for all to see.

My eyes started to well. I looked to my right and saw Donald. There was trepidation in his face, knowing it was for him, his mind inventing reasons why it couldn't be, and wondering if he was truly ready for that symbol so many have sacrificed for.

Donald was ready. He had already won Gracie Worlds and, in his last brown belt competition, submitted both opponents in less than a minute. Impressive.

His security work had also given him more real life experience using jiu jitsu than I ever had. He understood loyalty, respect, and what it meant to represent the art.

Burr Richards was an academy silverback who I made sure to invite that day. Burr was the oldest student I ever had, eventually bowing out in his sixties after his knees couldn't take anymore, sliding into a double replacement soon after. A lifelong martial artist, he made an astute prediction early on.

Years earlier, standing next to me on the mat, he looked over at D, and said "That's your first black belt right there."

I was surprised. Donald was a blue belt, while Jimmy was much more advanced.

I turned to Burr and asked, "Really? What about Jimmy?"

"Nah, that's your first black belt."

He was right. There's wisdom and experience in our elders. We forget that sometimes.

As I called up Donald to the center of the mat, emotion overcame him for a second as all of his dedication, preparation and disciplined study were represented in a single strip of cloth. He tied his new belt and it looked perfect on him.

My brother. My friend. I had become the black belt. Then I created one.

Under the guidance of my teacher, I completed the cycle.

I feel this was my finest moment.

Letting Go Completely

How you close is just an important as how you open.

Who wanted to take over? Donald was in graduate school out of town. Neil had other responsibilities. Paul, a brown belt who came to me under Ralph Gracie, was itching to step up to the plate. He was the same age as I was when I launched. I enjoyed seeing the parallels. I sold him everything, and extricated myself totally, in a clean positional escape.

Lots of people helped me start my venture, but it was Rick that really came through. I was happy to be able return the favor in stepping away, especially to such a loyal and dedicated jiu jitsu player like Paul. After some personnel changes in the dojo, enrollment had increased, and it felt good to hand over a healthy clientele as well as a turnkey business.

After so many years, your teaching chops get good. It's automatic really. So many classes, so many bodies, tailoring games for individuals based on all the physical factors.

Over time, you see physiques transform, confidence boosted, and lives reinvigorated through the work they put in on the mat.

There is no experience quite like it. As a martial artist, after a certain level is attained, the next field of growth is teaching. It's not just you anymore, and that forces you to expand your technical horizons.

Students may ask questions that surprise, frustrate, and even irritate you. Why? Because you may not know the answer immediately, or you can't verbalize it in that moment.

Some explanations require reflection, even though you're confident that it works based on your experience. This is where understanding deepens. This is where another level of learning takes place, where the student is the teacher.

Some yearn to grant this kind of experience. They want to develop warriors, fighters, and athletes of all ages. They want to have a hand in educating the public on physical literacy, and illustrate the power of distraction, angles and leverage.

They have a vision of the art they want to achieve, along with the opportunity to pass it on to others, stamped with their personal care and attention.

Those people should do it. If that's you, then you should do it.

Over the years I had talked to Brad several times about when the right moment to close would be. He always said, "You'll know when it's time." He was right. When the moment came, it was obvious. My lease was up, I was over it, and this was the moment to make room for something new.

I took the opportunity.

Leaving the academy for the last time, I flipped the off the lights and felt what that space meant to me.

I loved that Academy. I loved the people in it. Very few people realize what it took to keep it going. How much I poured out of my soul.

I stood in the darkness, in the embrace of my girlfriend, a Scandinavian princess named Kilee, saying goodbye to a dream.

You can only adjust your focus so many times before you need a new target. A new dream. A new path to the next level.

I was ready. I let go completely.

CHAPTER 23
WASH IT ALL AWAY

BEGINNERS MIND

WASH IT ALL AWAY

Jiu jitsu changes who you are. It gets you comfortable with change and appreciative of variation. Jiu jitsu allows you to look at people without fear or apprehension.

You can choose to approach situations indirectly, seeing how it's often easier to blend with others in order to achieve your goals.

But jiu jitsu also shows you how hold your ground, if the cause is right, or the situation requires it. You have that power too. You can move, or take a stand. It's your choice.

Jiu jitsu teaches you how to focus. How to get more accomplished with less effort. You start to see how the art advances your potential as a human being.

The bottom line is that it's a technology. A tool, which must be used correctly. Correct usage involves safety, control, and creating a culture where character development, empowerment and equality are encouraged.

We are adaptive creatures. Jiu jitsu keeps that spirit of adaptation alive and allows us to recognize the opportunities to act, while forging within us the courage to try.

The physical prowess you gain is one aspect of the journey. To bring jiu jitsu into your everyday life, however, now that's the real black belt test. Not just the competitions. It's harder to see this when you're young. But keep your eyes and ears open. Keep listening.

One day the words you heard long ago will finally sink in and you'll realize that the art is more than just an athletic outlet.

Now, as an instructor, I realize more than ever that teaching is about service, to your students, and to the art. Jiu jitsu allows us to magnify our potential. It's about the protection of self and your loved ones.

It's about humility. It's about compassion.

I never trained jiu jitsu for recognition or money. I did it because I loved it, because it was a constant companion in my life that allowed me to connect with others in a meaningful way.

There were some hard lessons on the path. If I could do it all over again, I'd give myself this advice: Don't take it personally. Be patient with others, as they're often giving you their best. And give your friends a pass, even if they're in the wrong.

Harbor no illusions. As skilled as I am, I still lose. This is the lifelong grounding that jiu jitsu gives you. That reality check. You are not invincible. You are a mortal being with finite energy. You may not feel that yet, but it's true. There are good days, but it's not always your day, and you will never stop paying your dues.

The discipline of jujutsu should serve your life. If it stops serving you, then make an adjustment in your relationship to it. Don't just do more.

More is not always the answer. Forward is not always the direction. Adjust yourself. Get your base. Correct the position.

The path will surely have some rocky terrain, so learn to be nimble, step around the obstacles in your path, and move forward in your journey. Move forward in your evolution.

To be able to read this book, on a plate of light and glass, is a miracle in one era, and the daily existence of another. We can change our minds, our bodies, our machines, our systems, our societies. It needn't be scary.

It's only scary if the approach is thoughtless, unintelligent, and without direction. Jujutsu teaches us how to become direct, intelligent and thoughtful. Starting on the mat. Then moving out into our lives.

So where do I go from here? I don't know. Which is the best part.

My training begins again.

ABOUT THE AUTHOR

Roy Dean is a martial artist, teacher, and author with over 30 years of experience in the arts. Holding a 4th degree black belt in Brazilian Jiu Jitsu and black belts in multiple other disciplines, Roy has dedicated his life to the study, practice, and teaching of martial arts.

He has trained and mentored students around the world, blending the traditions of classical martial arts with a modern approach to learning and self-development. His clear and methodical teaching style has made him a sought-after instructor, while his instructional videos and books have helped practitioners deepen their understanding of Jiu Jitsu and beyond.

He believes that martial arts are not just about technique, but also about developing character, discipline, and resilience—qualities that extend far beyond the mat.

Roy continues to teach, write, and evolve.

SNAPSHOTS OF THE JOURNEY

Age 17, with Judo master
Igami Shoten

My first hosts, the Uehara family,
in Toyokawa, Japan

Sparring as a fresh Judo shodan in Shoten's home dojo

United Gracie Tournament. San Francisco, California, 2000

First round triangle choke victory against a tough opponent

Brad Hirakawa, Phillip Palmejar with the gold medal, and myself

Scenes from the grappling class
at Jiai Aikido

Black belt exam. Mr. Harris allows me to attack

The pressure of the "BOA" must be felt to be believed

Roy Harris tying the belt around my waist, and
introducing me as a black belt

Nadija Alainentalo, Al Lowrimore, Roy Harris, myself,
Jeff Baldwin, Brad Hirakawa

3rd Street Dojo. Bend, Oregon, USA

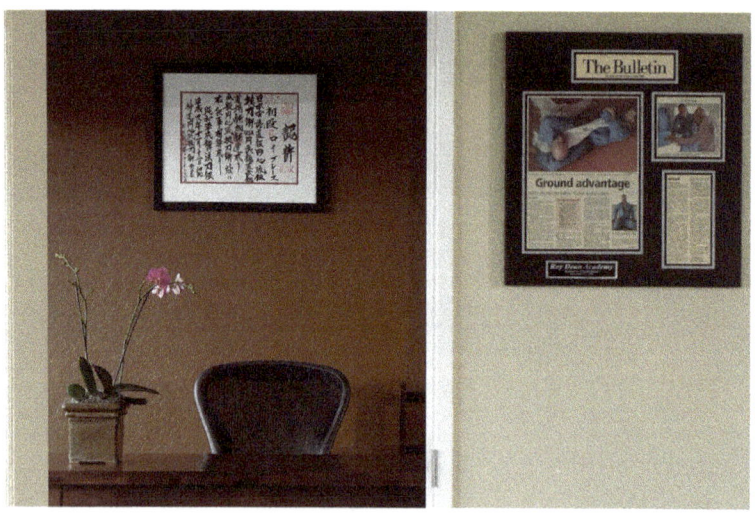

Academy office, with an article from the local newspaper

BECOMING THE BLACK BELT

Figure 4 armlock attack during an evening class

Early avatar. One of many iconic RDA jiu jitsu photos by Rick Ellis

Roy Harris, Donald Bowerman, and myself

The black belt is a peak experience for both teacher and student

BECOMING THE BLACK BELT

www.ingramcontent.com/pod-product-compliance
Lightning Source LLC
Chambersburg PA
CBHW051615120626
46551CB00014B/1806